The Rosary Will Make You a Saint

*America Needs Fatima dedicates this publication
to the memory of Mr. Antonio Fragelli,
a devoted promoter of Our Lady's Fatima
message and the Holy Rosary.*

The Rosary Will Make You a Saint

REV. FR. ÉDOUARD HUGON, O.P.

Originally published in French as:
Le Rosaire et la Sainteté
by

P. LETHIELLEUX 10, RUE CASSETTE PARIS FRANCE	LES ÉDITIONS DU LÉVRIER AV. NOTRE DAME DE GRÂCE, MONTRÉAL 95, AV. EMPRESS, OTTAWA CANADA

1948

— AMERICA NEEDS FATIMA —

APPROVAL

We have read, by order of the Very Reverend Father Provincial, a work by Rev. Fr. Édouard Hugon titled *Le Rosaire et la Sainteté*. It is an earnest yet brief study with beautiful and elevated doctrinal ideas and an exciting and almost new description of the rich graces contained in the Rosary. It will be useful reading for pious souls and even preachers, who will find in it ample spiritual nourishment.

Poitiers, France, July 19, 1900.

Fr. Denys Mézard, O.P., Fr. Henri Desqueyrous, O.P.

IMPRIMATUR
Fr. Joseph-Amb. Laboré
Prev. provinc. Occit. Lugdunensis

IMPRIMATUR
Parisiis, die 9 Augusti 1900
E. THOMAS
Vicaire général

To order more copies of this book, please contact:

America Needs Fatima
P.O. Box 341, Hanover, Penn. 17331
Tel.: (888) 317-5571
ANF@ANF.org · www.ANF.org

ISBN: 978-1-877905-66-7
Library of Congress Control Number: 2021950172

Printed in the United States of America

B109

Contents

"See, my daughter, My Heart surrounded with thorns with which ungrateful men pierce me at every moment with blasphemies and ingratitude. You, at least, make sure to console me..."

— *Our Lady to Lúcia, October 10, 1925.*

Foreword

The prophet Isaiah invites us to proclaim God's works known to His people. *Notes facite in populis ad inventiones eius.*[1] God's works! Human language is often unable to praise works of genius. But when it comes to divine works, we are lost in admiration and reduced to silence. Three among these works are so clearly divine that our minds cannot but bow to them. They are the Incarnation, the Divine Maternity, and the Eucharist.

After God's works, we find the works of Mary, all sublime and countless because they are works of love found in every age and among all peoples. One of her most excellent gifts is undoubtedly the Rosary, which St. Dominic's Order of Preachers made known worldwide. Since it became known in the thirteenth century, the Rosary has been a continuous song of praise and reassurance of a radiant future.

The institution of the Rosary is more than a work of genius, as in it, we find the supernatural wisdom that theologians admire in the institution of the Sacraments.

While we are far from equating the Rosary to the Sacraments, there are striking analogies between them. The Sacraments are in perfect harmony with human nature, which is both material and spiritual. To want man to apply purely intellectual acts would be to wean him in a way from milk indispensable to his happiness. His religion and worship need external nourishment. Like himself, his Sacraments must be composed of a soul and a body. The Sacraments have a body because they are sensible signs; they have a soul because they contain the invisible virtue of the Most High. The priest utters a few words, and suddenly,

---

[1] Isa. 12:4. "And you shall say in that day: Praise ye the Lord, and call upon his name: make his works known among the people: remember that his name is high."

the sign is invaded by divine majesty: through grace, God passes into the Sacraments; and at the same time that grace touches the soul, the soul touches God.

Likewise, true prayer engages the whole man. The Rosary, too, is composed of a soul and a body. The body of the Rosary is vocal prayer, and its soul is the meditation of each Mystery and the resulting spiritual strength. Like the Sacraments, the Rosary, as it were, has matter and form. It puts Our Lord's Sacred Humanity before our imagination and speaks to our physical nature. It sets the divinity of Christ before us by its sublime nature and thus appeals to our higher nature whereby we resemble angels and are like God Himself.

In the Sacraments, the words' outward sign and miraculous power combine to form only one thing, just as Christ's human nature and divine nature are united in one Person. In the Rosary, the vocal prayer and meditation on the Mystery form a single indivisible whole; to separate the form of the Sacrament from its matter is to destroy the Sacrament. To separate the Mystery from the vocal recitation is to destroy the very essence of the Rosary.

The Sacraments are like an extension and continuation of the Incarnation. They are like 'relics' of Our Lord. In the Sacraments, Jesus comes to bless us and save us. As in His time, He allows a healing power to escape from Him: "Virtue went out from Him and healed all."[2] Jesus comes to us as we say the Rosary so that, when announcing each Mystery, we can say that the Son of David is passing by, and pray: Son of David, have mercy on me.

The Sacraments are outward marks that distinguish a Christian from an infidel. The Rosary is the distinctive devotion of every true Catholic. The Sacraments are sweet but powerful bonds that unite the children of Christ. By partaking in the same Sacraments, the faithful show their communion in the same faith, hope, and love. Through the Rosary, Mary's knights unite throughout the world and join their voices, expressing their common hope and love. The Rosary is like a standard

---

[2] Luke 6:19. *Virtus de ille exibat et sanabat omnes.* "And all the multitude sought to touch him, for virtue went out from him, and healed all."

that God hoists before nations to assemble them from all corners of the universe. "He shall set up a standard unto the nations...and gather together the dispersed from the four quarters of the earth."[3]

It would be an easy task to delve deeper into this comparison between the Sacraments, established by Jesus, and the Rosary, a work of Mary. In a few words, humans need corporeal and sensible things to rise to spiritual things. The Sacraments and the Rosary are signs that raise the soul to contemplate eternal horizons, God, and eternity. Man craves spiritual nourishment and thirsts after the infinite, and the Sacraments and Rosary lead him to God. But this is only from a particular point of view: the Rosary has a somewhat unlimited scope.

Because of his physical nature and inherent weaknesses, man is a creature of time. However, the powers of his soul and his supernatural destiny also make him a creature of eternity. Well then, the Rosary is vast enough to embrace both time and eternity. It contains every age because it encompasses the unfathomable mysteries that underpin all history. Their realization constitutes what St. Paul calls the fullness of time: *plenitudo temporis*.[4] It encompasses eternity. The Rosary begins with heaven and eternity with the Mystery of the Incarnation and ends in heaven and eternity with the Mysteries of the Ascension of Jesus and the Crowning of Mary. We begin in the bosom of the Adorable Trinity and end in the bosom of the Blessed Virgin. From heaven to heaven, from eternity to eternity—here you have the expanses of the Rosary.

The Rosary is a summary of all Christianity and contains all that we believe. In the very first Mystery, we encounter the Blessed Trinity and the Incarnation. Like the Blessed Sacrament and Holy Mass, the Rosary is the memorial of Our Lord's life, Passion, Death, and Resurrection. In the Glorious Mysteries, we dwell on the truths of our last end in a striking but practical way. The Rosary is the theology that prays, adores, and proclaims in each dogma: Glory be to the Father, to the Son, and to the Holy Spirit.

---

[3]   Isa. 11:12. *Elevabit signum in nationibus . . . et . . . colliget a quatuor plagis terrae.*
[4]   Gal. 4:4.

In a sense, this great devotion summarizes moral theology, which deals with sin and virtue. You cannot truly realize the infinite malice of mortal sin unless you see—by meditating on the Sorrowful Mysteries—divine justice falling upon the innocent Christ and requiring that He pay the frightful ransom of the Cross to the point that He had to cry out, under the weight of our sins, "My God, My God, why hast Thou forsaken Me?" For us, each of these Mysteries contains a sublime lesson of virtue. More than mere examples of heroism, they are the very summits of the mystical life. Accordingly, the Rosary is moral theology that prays, weeps, expiates, and rises to heroism while crying out to Christ: "Thou hast redeemed us to God in Thy Blood, and hast made us to our God a kingdom and priests."[5]

In the Rosary, we find a recapitulation of all history, as its object is He to Whom all history points, Whose radiant figure dominates both the Old and New Testaments. Once again, the Rosary is history that prays and leads all nations to Christ, saying: Thou art the Alpha and Omega, the beginning and the end.

As Pope Leo XIII eloquently proved, the Rosary has even solved the social question:[6] Why are nations in fear and societies troubled? The Sovereign Pontiff says the answer is threefold. The first cause is a growing dislike of a simple and laborious life, the remedy for which one finds in the Joyful Mysteries. The second cause is repugnance to any suffering, for which one finds the medicine in the Sorrowful Mysteries. The third cause is the forgetfulness of our ultimate life and destiny, the object of our hope, and the Glorious Mysteries contain the remedy for this evil. Once again, the Rosary answers the social question with that cry of victory: *Christus vincit, Christus regnat, Christus imperat!* Christ conquers, Christ reigns, Christ rules!

Thus, we see the marvelous way the Rosary can adapt itself to every condition, every age, every people. It is so simple to pray

---

[5]   Apoc. 5:9-10. *Redemisti nos Deo in sanguine tuo, et fecisti nos Deo nostro regnum et sacerdotes.*

[6]   Encyclical *Laetitiae Sanctae*, recommending devotion to the Rosary, September 8, 1893.

and meditate that anyone can do it, no matter how uneducated or illiterate. Indeed, it was once called the psalter of the unlearned. On the other hand, its Mysteries are so profound as to make it the inexhaustible *Summa* of theologians. Consequently, it is the grand synthesis of Christianity. From beginning to end, all is included in the fifteen Mysteries of the Rosary, just as time is encompassed by the two shores of eternity.

It would be interesting to compare the Rosary with the *Summa Theologiae* of St. Thomas and the Christian churches of the Middle Ages.

All three are, in their way, a compendium of Christianity. Each is, so to speak, a poem that unfolds before our eyes the wondrous plan of the Almighty. Each is a monumental pedestal that has withstood the onslaught of the ages and brings us closer to God and the supernatural. Each is quickened by the same divine life. In the *Summa*, in ancient cathedrals, in the Rosary, the soul experiences unfathomable joy and contentment, feeling closer to its true home—heaven and God. Dominated by Christ, St. Thomas, the cathedral, and the Rosary form a triple synthesis, a triple teaching, and a triple song of love and acknowledgment of the same God and Savior.

The first two are examples of human genius, but the Rosary is more than that because it contains supernatural wisdom. In a word, it is the work of Our Lady.

Although we should study this great devotion in detail, here we want to outline its most important points and show how the Rosary summarizes all the works of God.

One can sum up the work of the Almighty in two words: Creation and Redemption. Both comprise all the marvels of things real and ideal. The Almighty will be able to rest when His two ambitions see completion. God rested after six days in the work of creation, not because His omnipotence was exhausted but that He might contemplate His work and see that it was good. *Et vidit Deus quod esset bonum.*[7] However, to carry out the work of redemption, the Almighty waited for a long time, as if allowing Himself to be overcome with fatigue.

---

[7]   Gen. 1:10.

According to St. Augustine and St. Thomas, crowning a soul with glory or even endowing it with the gift of grace is, in one sense, an action greater than creating heaven and earth. We intend to show how the Rosary sums up this miracle of grace and holiness. This devotion reveals to us the Author of holiness. It shows us our models in the way of perfection and teaches us how to practice virtue. Jesus is the Author of holiness. Now, to know the God-Man, we must study His Heart, Soul, and Divinity; and the Rosary is the book that will teach us all this.

After Jesus, our models in holiness are Mary and St. Joseph, who cooperated with Him in the work of redemption. The Rosary makes us appreciate their proper role in the economy of salvation. The practice of holiness comprises the whole of Christian perfection from simple charity to heroic charity. The Rosary initiates us and gradually brings us to ever-higher degrees in the spiritual life.

Therefore, our work has three parts:

1. The Rosary and Jesus, the Author of sanctity.

2. The Rosary and Mary and Joseph, models of holiness.

3. The Rosary and the practice of holiness.

This booklet is not a profound doctrinal study, nor do we intend to delve into aspects of the Rosary that several learned writers have already covered extensively. We are simply offering some theological and pious considerations that will help people in their spiritual life. We also deal with this subject from a single viewpoint not to repeat what other writings on the Rosary have said. Fulfilling the wishes of some friends, we so arranged the chapters that each may form an independent meditation by itself, even though all are logically connected. That explains and justifies repetitions in certain places. May this booklet make the Virgin of the Rosary and her Divine Son better known and loved.

Part One

The Rosary and the Author of Sanctity: Jesus, His Heart, Soul, and Divinity

Statue of the Sacred Heart of Jesus at the altar used by
St. John Bosco shortly before his death. Museum of the
Home of St. John Bosco, Turin, Italy.

Chapter One

The Rosary and the Sacred Heart of Jesus

Without diminishing the integrity of His essence, God, Who is infinite perfection and purity, absolute sanctity, beauty ever ancient and new, has shared His divine attributes with created beings to some degree. He gave us the ability to recognize and admire perfections reflected in creatures.

We can distinguish two types of beauty in creatures: sublime beauty and gracious beauty. One sees gracious beauty, for instance, in light, flowers, and all things that delight and enchant us. We see sublime beauty in vast oceans, lofty mountains, and boundless skies. However, nowhere is gracious beauty more worthy of admiration than in a human heart, the heart of a child, a virgin, or a devoted friend. The poetry of the heart is the sweetest and most agreeable. The depths and sublimity of the ocean have often been compared with the depths and sublimity of the heart. Which is harder to fathom, the deep sea or a human heart? One cannot speak of sublimity without considering the human heart and particularly the hearts of mothers and saints.

When forming the heart of the first man, God had before Him a model, an ideal: the Heart of Christ. As Tertullian put it, *Christus cogitabatur homo futurus:* "In His mind was present Christ, the Man to come." How sweet it is to remember that on the day of our creation God modeled our hearts on that of His Son!

Therefore, in order to know all the marvels of our world, we must know the human heart. Now, to know the most perfect and ideal human heart, we must delve into the depths of the

4

Sacred Heart of Jesus. If we wish to admire graciousness with all its charms, we must contemplate the Divine Heart of Our Lord. We must enter into His Sacred Heart, of which it has been written: "Thou art beautiful above the sons of men; grace is poured abroad in thy lips."[1] If we want to admire sublimity in all its beauty and understand, as St. Paul says,[2] something of the graciousness and sublimity found in the Heart of Jesus, we must study His Heart.

The Rosary reveals to us the graciousness and sublimity of the Sacred Heart of Jesus.

It would be wrong to consider the Sacred Heart in an abstract manner separated from the Person of Christ, an error that theologians have condemned. The Rosary is the true revelation of the Sacred Heart because it always represents it united to the Divinity, from which the Heart can never be separated. Saying the Rosary, we can contemplate that living and beating Heart in the time, places, and circumstances in which Our Lord lived. We can consider the sentiments of His Adorable Heart toward His Eternal Father, toward men, and Himself. In the Joyful Mysteries, it is a heart full of love and tenderness. In the Sorrowful Mysteries, it is a heart inebriated with love and overwhelmed with bitterness. In the Glorious Mysteries, it is a heart still enraptured with love but exalted in its triumph. In the Joyful Mysteries, it is a gracious beauty. In the Sorrowful and Glorious Mysteries, it is sublime beauty.

We have said that graciousness is admirable above all in the heart of a child. On the day of our baptism, our parents looked lovingly into our cradle and echoed those words of joy: "Let us rejoice, for a child is born unto us, a man is born into the world." *Natus est homo in mundum.*[3] The heavenly family leaned still more lovingly over the same cradle, saying, "A God is born unto us, let us rejoice, a God is born to us!" Grace made us children of God. That tiny heart that had only just begun to throb was the temple of the Blessed Trinity. As a poet beautifully put it, the angels contemplate their image in the cradle.

---

[1]   Ps. 44:3. Speciosus forma præ filiis hominum, diffusa est gratia in labiis tuis.
[2]   Eph. 3:18.
[3]   2 John 16:21.

Now, what are any baby's attractions next to the charms of the Heart of the Infant God in the cradle of Bethlehem? St. Paul says that "the grace of God our Savior has appeared to all men"— *Apparuit gratia Dei Salvatoris nostri.*[4] How touching, innocent, and gracious were the glorious events of that Christmas night! As the angels sang, the shepherds visited that cradle that sheltered Him Who came to redeem the world! How wonderful it would be to see, depicted in a single picture, all the events that accompanied the birth of Jesus!

That picture exists: it is the Rosary. The Mystery of the Nativity is the principal scene, around which the others are secondary scenes. There, the Infant Jesus reveals His Heart with all its graces: *Apparuit gratia Dei Salvatoris nostri.*[5] Poetry alone can express these ravishing charms, which St. Alphonsus Liguori sang in one of his Canticles:

> "Mary sings, the ravished heavens
> Hush the music of their spheres;
> Soft her voice, her beauty fairer
> Than the glancing stars appear;
> While to Jesus, slumbering nigh,
> Thus she sings her lullaby:
>
> "Sleep, my Babe, my God, my Treasure,
> Gently sleep; but ah! the sight
> With its beauty so transports me,
> I am dying with delight;
> Thou canst not Thy mother see,
> Yet Thou breathest flames to me.
>
> "If within your lids unfolded,
> Slumbering eyes, Thou seemest so fair;
> When upon my gaze Thou doth open,
> How shall I Thy beauty bear?
> Ah! I tremble when Thou wake,
> Lest my heart with love should break.

---

4   Titus 2:11.
5   Idem. "For the grace of God our Savior hath appeared to all men."

"Cheeks than sweetest roses sweeter,
Mouth where lurks a smile Divine,
Though the kiss my Babe should waken,
I must press those lips to mine.
Pardon, Dearest, if I say
Mother's love will take no nay.

"As she ceased, the gentle Virgin
Clasped the Infant to her breast,
And, upon His radiant forehead
Many a loving kiss impressed.
Jesus woke and on her face
Fixed a look of heavenly grace.

"Ah! that look, those eyes, that beauty,
How they pierce the Mother's heart!
Shafts of love from every feature
Through her gentle bosom dart.
Heart of stone! can I behold
Mary's love, and still be cold?

"Where, my soul, thy sense, thy reason?
When will these delays be o'er?
All things else, how fair so ever,
Are but smoke: resist no more!
Yes! 'tis done! I yield my arms
Captive to those double charms.

"If, alas, O heavenly beauty!
Now so late those charms I learn,
Now at least, and ever, ever
With thy love my heart will burn,
For the Mother and the Child,
Rose and Lily undefiled."[6]

---

6   The Madonna's Lullaby, http://www.catholictradition.org/Christmas/christmas-hymn2.htm.

The beauty of graciousness reveals itself in the hearts of virgins whose every sigh is for their God. Mary is the first beauty, the first virgin. Assuredly, the Heart of Jesus is the immaculate Model of all things virginal. He is the Virgin God, the Son of a Virgin Mother, and the Spouse of a virgin Church. How beautiful! Holy souls fully understand it. Enchanted with this pure ideal, they long to offer up their hearts on the chaste breast of Jesus and taste, close to Him, the austere delights of charity. By your charms and beauty, O Divine Spouse of Virgins, reign in the hearts of all men!

Finally, gracious beauty manifests itself in a friend's heart: *Amicus fidelis medicamentum vitae*—"A faithful friend is the medicine of life," says the Holy Spirit.[7] He works as a balm in your life, shares all your joys and sorrows, and wipes away your tears. Now, God, Whom we honor with the Rosary, is our friend of friends, Who remains when all others leave. Friendship can exist only between equals. In the first Mysteries of the Rosary, God makes Himself our equal by assuming our nature and giving us His own. In every Mystery, we feel the pulsations of a friend's loving heart. We recognize the tender voice of a friend when Jesus smiles at the shepherds and Magi, when He instructs the doctors and unlearned, and when He deigns to speak those consoling words: "Come to Me, all of you who labor and are burdened, and I will refresh you."[8] His is the loving and devoted Heart whose delights are to be with the children of men. Let us no longer dwell on the graciousness of the Sacred Heart. More than words, pious meditations on the Mysteries of the Rosary will enable us to delight in its charms.

Let us now consider, in the Sacred Heart of Jesus, beauty that is sublime and heroic. When heroism appears, nature is overcome as it were, and one feels that God is present. The seeds of heroism, which are gifts from the Holy Spirit, are sown in the hearts of all the just. When circumstances so require, these supernatural energies go into action, and heroism spontaneously arises like a flower from the seed. That is why a mother's heart is capable of sublime and noble deeds, and a

---

[7] Ecclus. 6:16.
[8] Matt. 2:28.

saint's life is, as it were, filled with heroism. Theologians teach that all virtues were found in Jesus Christ from the very first moment of His conception and attained in Him their full perfection. He practiced them to a heroic degree—the most perfect possible—and His heroism was divine. The perfect virtues that adorned His soul have overflowed from His heart to the world so that He might manifest His Heart to us. Thus, we can say that He constantly lived a life of heroism in every one of His Mysteries, both laying in the manger and hanging on the Cross. Naturally, this heroism is more evident in the Sorrowful Mysteries than in the other Mysteries.

Can you imagine a scene more mysterious, more heart rendering and sublime than the agony of Jesus? If one were to gather the most poignant anguish, the bitterest sorrows, the most painful sacrifices, the most admirable devotedness that moves a human heart, one would have top-notch heroism and an ocean of affliction. That would give us an idea of the anguish of a dying man but not the unfathomable agony of the heart of a dying God.

What is it that renders this Mystery so sublime? It is the sacrifice of love rejected and unheeded. Jesus knew that He would be misunderstood, despised, and persecuted. He heard in advance the painful echo of the voice of peoples, saying, love is unloved; love is detested. Yet, the love of the Heart of Jesus cries out more loudly than all the impious insults and sacrileges He suffered at the hands of men and demons. His tears cry out, but above all, His love cries out (*Clamant lacrymae, sed super omnia clamat amor*).

We see the same heroism in the Scourging at the Pillar, the Crowning with Thorns, the Carrying of the Cross. We hear at the Praetorium, in the streets of Jerusalem, on the way to Calvary, the cries of the crowd, the insults of the executioners. Above all, we hear the voice of sublimity: *Clamant lacrymae, sed super omnia clamat amor*, "O Jesus, your tears cry out, your wounds cry out, but above all, your love cries out."

Finally, God and death come face to face on Golgotha. God and death! What a solemn and awesome encounter! There, it is God Who wants to be the conquered one. Yet death, seemingly triumphant, only earns Jesus an even more glorious title: God, Almighty, and creative Love, now has a new name: the Victim of Love.

The Crucifixion of Jesus is the perfection of sublimity because it is love made perfect by the full consummation of the sacrifice. The still remaining drops of blood in the Heart of the Divine Crucified must also be shed! Soldier, come and open this Heart! He does, and immediately there came forth blood and water (*Et continuo exivit sanguis et aqua*).[9] Now, there is nothing left to give. The sacrifice is complete, showing the perfection of love in the perfect sacrifice of the God-Man. Thus, sublimity predominates throughout the Passion of Jesus: a divine sublimity, the depths of which no man or creature can fathom.

God and death again come face to face in the Mystery of the Resurrection, but this time, it is God Who is the conqueror. The Heart of Jesus, having submitted heroically to the ignominy of the tomb, is now sublimely triumphant over death and hell to bestow on us His divine life. The last Mysteries take place in heaven, in the sublimity of eternal glory. Silence is now required as we enter into celestial regions and recall those words of St. Paul: "Eye hath not seen, nor ear heard, neither hath it entered into the heart of man, what things God hath prepared for them that love Him."[10]

Here we see how admirably the Heart of Jesus encompasses all the beauty and magnificence of graciousness and sublimity, which the Rosary reveals to us. It is even more reason for us to contemplate and honor this Divine Heart by meditating on the Mysteries of the Rosary so that He Who is their source and plenitude may grant us abundant graces through the intercession of His Immaculate Mother.

---

[9] John 19:34.
[10] 1 Cor. 2:9.

Slovakian lithograph print of the Crucifixion of Jesus with the Virgin Mary and Saint John the Evangelist.

Chapter Two

The Rosary and the Soul
and Knowledge of Jesus

Let us delve even deeper into the Heart of Jesus. Deeper than the abysses of the heart are the abysses of the soul. Yet, even deeper than the abysses of the soul, we will discover those of the divinity. The Rosary leads us into the depths of the deep; from the depths and abysses of the heart into the depths and abysses of the soul; from the depths and abysses of the soul into the depths and abysses of the divinity.

For starters, let us enter the holy soul of Our Savior, that masterpiece in which God united all perfections of the human and angelic worlds. In a word, the riches of these two worlds are knowledge or truth and holiness or grace. The realm of the spirit is a realm of enlightenment. Knowledge is as a fire kindled at the summit of one's intellect. Truth is the splendor that crowns that radiant summit. Yet, a will transfigured by grace is incomparably more magnificent and noble than knowledge. This transfiguration is holiness, produced by grace.

Therefore, grace and truth are the common treasures of the two intellectual worlds. We will show how the knowledge and grace of Jesus Christ surpassed the knowledge and grace of the angels and humanity combined. *Plenum gratiae et veritatis:*[1] "He is full of grace and truth."

Let us try to study, albeit in a summary way, the science and grace of Our Lord.

St. Paul says that in Christ are hidden all treasures of wisdom

---

[1]   John 1:14.

and knowledge (*In quo sunt omnes thesauri sapientae et scientiae absconditi*).[2] If a single mind could possess all the knowledge and understanding of man and angel together, it would surely be an incredible treasure. Yet, it would be impossible to fathom the depths of that mind—as deep as an ocean, but not a bottomless abyss.

It is impossible to fathom the depths of Jesus Christ. When exploring an abyss, new depths unceasingly succeed those already discovered; the same happens concerning the knowledge of the Word Incarnate. New hidden depths always follow those we endeavor to fathom so that it would be impossible to discover all those hidden treasures.

Distinct from His infinite knowledge as God, in the soul of Our Lord, there are three kinds of knowledge: beatific, infused, and experimental. From the very first instant of His creation, He was able to gaze on the infinite with the eyes of His soul. He was able to contemplate God face-to-face, enraptured with that torrent of delights that finds its source in eternity. Since all glory derives from Christ, it was proper for Him to possess what He intended to bestow on others. He, therefore, enjoyed glory from His very conception.

By His beatific knowledge, the soul of the Word knew the past, the present, and the future. As the absolute Master of heaven and earth, it is only fitting that He should know everything that happens throughout His Empire. As the Judge of the living and the dead, He must be aware of everything that will be brought to His tribunal: our every action, innermost thoughts, and the most secret movements of our hearts. Present to Him shall be all that is, has been, and will be.

Meditating on the Rosary will bring all these thoughts to our minds. For example, in the Mystery of the Annunciation, we may ponder: Jesus Christ knows me, thinks of me, reads all my thoughts, and sees all my feelings. He knows all my ingratitude and still loves me, offers me His Heart, and gently calls me by name. He kindly receives my adoration, affection, and desires, seeing me enrolled in the grand army of the Rosary.

---

[2]   Col. 2:3.

He knew in advance the act of love I would make to Him as I recite this decade, and He thanked me in advance. We can continue meditating on the other Mysteries in the same way.

Thus, the Rosary will lead us into the very soul of Jesus, who knows everything we will tell Him. He knows what we were doing before our prayers and sees how we are saying them. He also knows what we intend to do when we are finished. We will do our best to remain in His presence in an attitude of utmost respect and burning love and strive to avoid everything that might offend Him. We should bear in mind that we speak to a blessed Soul Who can and wants to bestow on us the gift of eternal bliss. So, in each Mystery, let us say to Him: O holy soul of my Savior, for the sake of your joys, sufferings, and triumphs, help me to attain the beatific vision to be wholly united to You!

In the second place, the soul of Christ has infused knowledge as the one implanted in angelic intellects. Men need to acquire knowledge from the world around them. While the truth is the manna of the soul, we must gather it little by little and only with arduous labor from the vast fields of creation. Not so with angels: the "manna" falls directly into their minds. From their very inception, God infused in them such powerful ideas and insights that the entire universe is wide open to their gaze.

It would be unbecoming for Christ, King of the angels, to lack a perfection that enriches His subjects. From the very dawn of its creation, His soul was infused with knowledge incomparably broader and vaster than that of the angels. With their innate knowledge, the angels know everything about the works of nature but nothing about the decrees of the Divine Will. They know neither the future nor the secrets of hearts. By its infused knowledge, the soul of the Word was aware of everything concerning the gift of wisdom and prophecy: the past, the present, the future, and the secrets of hearts. In short, His infused knowledge of creation is as universal as His beatific knowledge.

By introducing us into the sanctuary of Christ's soul, the Rosary makes us in some way participants in His infused knowledge. It initiates us into the marvelous Mysteries that the angels learned only little by little. In a few moments, it teaches us more about supernatural truths than was revealed to the angels during the long centuries that preceded the Incarnation. All revelations and prophecies of the Old Testament are, as it were, contained and realized in the Rosary. While reciting a few decades, our field of vision covers the entire supernatural order.

Privileged souls, who delve deeper into this meditation, sometimes receive heavenly communications as their entrance into the soul of Christ enlightens them with His light and enables them to understand His secrets. Infused knowledge is not a rare occurrence in the annals of holiness, and many saints received it by meditating on the Mysteries of the Rosary.

While we do not aspire to these extraordinary favors, from the moment we unite our souls with that of Our Redeemer, we all have the right to hope for the grace of illumination to understand better the truths on which we meditate. Supernatural light will radiate from the Divine Soul, making the profundities of these Mysteries intelligible for us. Reciting our dear Rosary will strengthen our souls and make us participants in the infused knowledge of Christ.

Finally, we must consider Our Lord's acquired or experimental knowledge. His two higher forms of knowledge did not hinder the natural activity of His intellect. From a purely human point of view, Jesus Christ is the greatest genius the world has seen and will ever see. Being the perfect representative of humanity, His soul encompasses everything that is creative and fertile in the soul of a poet, all that is pure and ideal in the soul of an artist, and all that is noble and generous in that of an orator. Compared to Him, other geniuses are as children next to a giant or an obscure planet before the sun. His penetrating mind pierces the essence of things, taking it all in with a single glance. He easily acquired experimental knowledge that costs us so much labor and fatigue.

Simply by His acquired knowledge, He knew all truths that reason can understand. He scrutinized all secrets of nature. He saw in advance all the marvelous inventions of which the human mind is capable. His own master, He is the Teacher of angels and men and learned from no one.

Perfect from the beginning, both His beatific and infused

knowledge remained invariable. However, His experimental knowledge underwent real progress. St. Thomas says we must take these words of the Gospel literally: "Jesus advanced in wisdom and age."[3] His understanding continuously developed until it attained its perfection.

Now, Our Lord acquired this knowledge by each of His acts and in the main events of His life, which we recall in the Joyful Mysteries. Thus, meditating on the Rosary brings us into contact with His experimental knowledge, and so we can hope that Jesus, our Teacher, will help us acquire the knowledge necessary for our state in life. If our vocation requires that we devote ourselves to study, the Psalter of Mary will give us a mighty help. As we recite a few Aves (Hail Marys) and delve into the depths of Christ, our work becomes easier and more fruitful. Like Jesus, we advance quickly in knowledge and wisdom. Some of the world's most celebrated geniuses resorted to the Rosary when needing inspiration. To this day, two large rosaries that belonged to Michelangelo, and appear to have been used frequently, are on display. Joseph Haydn famously stated, "When my composition starts to falter, I pace my room up and down, Rosary in hand, and say some Hail Marys, and soon my ideas come back."

Happy is a study thus conducted. Blessed are the moments spent united with the adorable soul of Him who is the Creator of geniuses and saints!

---

[3]   Luke 2:52.

The Finding of the Child Jesus in the Temple.
Church of the Sacred Heart of Jesus, São Paulo, Brazil.

Chapter Three

The Rosary and the Soul of Jesus, His Grace

The Rosary unveils to us the threefold knowledge of the Word Incarnate. However, to have a complete revelation of His soul, we must consider its fullness of grace (*plenum gratiae*). Grace, above all, is what produces beauty in beings. A saint once remarked that if we could see a soul in the state of grace, we would die of wonder and joy. St. Thomas says that restoring a sinner to grace is, in a sense, an action greater than creating heaven and earth.[1] Accordingly, to describe the beauties of grace is to describe the splendors of the soul of Jesus. We are unable to surmise the treasures of this adorable soul unless we realize the value of grace. That is why we will broadly strive to describe the marvelous operations of grace in the soul of Our Savior. We will then show how the Rosary communicates the grace of Christ to us.

Grace is a heavenly gift that makes us God-like supernatural beings and the abode of God Himself. It widens our nature's narrow confines and raises us above humanity and even the angelic nature.

Had the angels not been given grace, they would be on a lower plane than man. In heaven, the saints who have attained a greater degree of grace than the angels will overtake them in glory.

If God had created more perfect beings than even the Seraphim (without endowing them with the gift of grace), one would have to exclaim, go higher! as they would still not be on

---

[1] *Summa Theologiae, Prima Secundae*, q. 113, art. IX.

the supernatural level.

The supernatural is a second nature added to our first nature and raises us to the level of God Himself. We have a soul in the natural order and a soul in the supernatural order. St. Augustine says that grace is the soul of our soul. In the natural order, we have faculties: intellect, will, and sensibility. In the supernatural order, our faculties are the infused virtues: first, the theological virtues, rooted in God Himself; then, the cardinal virtues with their various divisions; higher up, the gifts of the Holy Spirit, which implant the seeds of heroism in us. That is not all. The virtues and gifts are crowned by the twelve fruits of the Holy Spirit and the evangelical beatitudes. In short, such is the marvelous supernatural framework. At the foundation is grace; then, the infused virtues; higher, the seven gifts; even higher, the twelve fruits of the Holy Spirit; and at the very pinnacle, the evangelical beatitudes.

Yet, we still have hardly said anything. Grace actually makes us divine, God-like. *Ego dixi, dii estis*—"I have said: You are gods."[2] If we could penetrate the souls of the just, we would see divine characteristics—so to speak, an image of God. As the Holy Doctors of the Church teach, grace is a bright mirror where God contemplates Himself. Now God cannot recognize Himself except in what is divine. If we are mirrors of the Lord, we should reflect His divine traits. Hence, as we salute a soul in the state of grace, let us inwardly salute the image of God! *Divinae consortes naturae*, says St. Peter:[3] "Grace makes us partakers of the divine nature."

When plunged into a furnace, gold takes on the color, heat, and flame of fire while at the same time retaining all its properties. As grace plunges him into the divine essence, man is filled with God without ceasing to be human! He thinks in God, acts in God, loves in God. Kings are proud of their royal lineage. The royal and divine blood of Jesus Christ flows in the veins of all the righteous just as a vine transmits life and growth even to its furthermost offshoots. The heroes of pagan antiquity wanted to be seen as children of some god. For them,

---

[2]   Ps. 81:6.

[3]   2 Pet. 1:4.

that was a sacrilegious fable; for us, it is reality. Our genealogy is truly celestial, as we can say with St. Paul, *Genus sumus Dei*: "We are the offspring of God."[4] This is our claim to nobility, of which we can be proud.

Finally, grace gives us the very Person of God Himself. Theologians call this hallowed mystery the indwelling of the Blessed Trinity in the soul.

By an invisible anointing, grace consecrates our soul and makes it into a temple in which God delights. *Vos estis Templum Dei Vivi*: "You are the temple of the Living God," says St. Paul.[5] St. Bernard says that the ceremonies of baptism resemble very closely those prescribed for the consecration of a church. Now, one builds a temple or church precisely for God to dwell in it. The Three Divine Persons come into the soul and make their abode in it. *Ad eum veniemus et mansionem apud eum faciemus.*[6] Thus, the Trinity is truly present in the souls of the just. As the altar chalice really contains the Blood of Jesus, so our souls possess the Holy Spirit. Both the altar chalice and the chalice of a holy soul shelter God.

The indwelling of the Trinity is the presence of a friend with a friend, a spouse with a spouse. When in need, we do not have to go far to find a consoler. We just need to enter the sanctuary of our soul: the Three Divine Persons are always there to alleviate our sorrows and wipe our tears. They enlighten our intellect and make us see everything from the standpoint of eternity, to see only the divine plan being fulfilled in all events of life. Scripture says, *Ecce Dominus transit!* "Behold, the Lord is passing!"[7] They transform our will to perceive God's will in whatever befalls us. Even trials and death become a beverage we drink with eagerness and delight. *Gustara mortem* (taste of death).

Finally, the Three Divine Persons also transfigure our bodies. The bodies of the saints possess a secret beauty, a

---

4   Acts 17:28-29.
5   2 Cor. 6:16.
6   John 14:23. "Jesus answered, and said to him: If any one love me, he will keep my word, and my Father will love him, and we will come to him, and will make our abode with him."
7   3 Kings 19:2.

hidden splendor that at times appears at the hour of death. A kind of divine majesty will protect our dust even in the tomb. Our members, even in corruption, bear as it were an invisible inscription that they once were the temple of the Trinity—they are sacred until the resurrection.

While speaking of grace, we have not strayed from the consideration of Our Lord because all the treasures of grace abound in His soul. In Him, one finds to an eminent degree all the supernatural wonders we have touched on. His blessed soul was flooded with torrents of grace from the very first instant of His creation. The closer one is to a source, the more water one draws from it. The closer we draw to a furnace, the more we feel its heat. The Divinity is the source and ocean of grace, the home and sun of love. Is it possible to be more united to God than was the soul of Our Redeemer? The Divinity and His most holy soul were united in an embrace so ineffable and intimate that only one Person resulted from it. In that ocean of grace, His soul was flooded and filled even to overflowing— *plenum gratiae* (full of grace). You cannot add to overflowing fullness. When an abyss is full, what can you add to it?

In the soul of the Word, under the influence of grace, all virtues expanded and blossomed forth into the exquisite flower of heroism. Vices, which belong to the state of imperfection, found no place in that garden. Conversely, there blossomed, as if on virgin soil fertilized by the sun of eternity, all the natural virtues, infused virtues, gifts and fruits of the Holy Spirit, the power of miracles, and the gift of prophecy. All the beauty that God placed in nature and grace, He gathered in the soul of Jesus. If we could see that soul, we would be ecstatic with admiration and love. While God reserves this rapture for eternity, the Rosary can give us a foretaste of it.

In order to get a true picture of a soul, we must study it and look at all the circumstances that will likely bring out its inner workings. Now, what circumstances reflect more clearly the depths of the soul of Jesus than those recalled in the Mysteries of the Rosary? He grew in grace, says the Gospel, meaning that His grace displayed marvelous effects and radiated in each of those Mysteries through the transparent veil of His flesh. It was enough to see Jesus working, speaking, and teaching to catch a glimpse of the brightness of that hidden grace. Likewise, as we silently meditate on the Rosary, the soul of Christ passes before our eyes. His grace shines once again through the Mystery, makes His presence felt, and draws us closer to Him. The Rosary is the living revelation of the soul of Christ and its divine riches.

Above all, we would like to show how the Rosary concretely applies the grace of Our Redeemer to us. The grace Christ received established Him as the spiritual head of all humanity and made Him capable of bestowing grace upon us. We do not receive a single supernatural good that is not derived from this first principle. Jesus is the great reservoir, the vast ocean of grace whence all men must draw if they wish to be saved. We draw from this ocean unceasingly, and it always remains full. Now, by each of His Mysteries, the Word's humanity merited this grace for us. Thus, we see how meditation on the Rosary brings us into contact with the source of our salvation by establishing communication between Christ and us. His divine life pours abundantly upon our souls. Each Mystery, says one holy Doctor, is like a fruitful breast from which flows the milk of grace. So to speak, when reciting the decades, we drink the milk of heaven.

Undoubtedly, we must be careful to avoid exaggerations. We are not saying that the Rosary applies sanctifying grace directly to our souls, as do the Sacraments. Such efficacy is not proper to the Rosary or any other devotion. It would be an error to claim that its recitation suffices of itself to give us an increase of grace. However, it is no illusion to believe that by piously uniting ourselves with the Mysteries that worked our salvation, God will grant us many actual graces. As the Gospel says, it sufficed to touch our Savior's garments to be healed.

When saying each Mystery, are we not touching, as it were, a fold of Jesus' mantle? Have we not a right to hope that a virtue that heals will escape from it? *Virtus de illo exibat et sanabat omnes.*[8] The Mystery that expiated our sins of pride will help

---

[8] Luke 6:19. "And all the multitude sought to touch him, for virtue went out from him, and healed all."

especially in the practice of humility. The Mystery that expiated impure vice will help us to practice the virtue of chastity, and likewise with the other Mysteries.

Our Lord is a magnificent sun that enlightens every man coming into this world. The Rosary exposes us to His heat and light. In the Mysteries of the Annunciation and Nativity, we watch the rising sun of justice. While meditating on the Glorious Mysteries, we contemplate that sun at noon, in all its glory. Its rays beam down on us, and we reflect its brilliance. The fire of divinity rekindles our souls, turning us into fire and love, like God. How quickly we would advance in the spiritual life if we only knew how to profit by this devotion!

The greatest saints of the Order of St. Dominic found the secret of their holiness in the Rosary. Brother M. Raphael Meysson, O.P., of holy memory, used to call the Rosary "the secret of holiness."[9] Hidden in the adorable soul of their God, they drank deeply from the source of grace. They obtained a little of that heroism that detaches us from the earth and experienced a bit of that ineffable rapture that is a foretaste of heaven. Like these privileged souls, may we descend every day into the depths of the soul of our Beloved, source of salvation and happiness! The enemy can never violate this sanctuary. The onslaughts of hell, which find easy access into worldly-minded souls, will never break into those luminous and always serene depths.

---

[9] Read the very edifying work titled *Vie intérieure*, by Fr. Marie Raphael, Paris, Librairie Ch. Poussielgue.

"And He was transfigured before them. And His face did shine as the sun: and His garments became white as snow."
(Matt. 17:3)

Chapter Four

The Rosary and the Divinity of Jesus

To dwell in the soul of the Word is to live in a region far removed from the hustle and bustle—a serene Mount Tabor, a summit close to the heaven of heavens. By reflecting the splendor of this soul, we progress in the knowledge of Christ; it is the illuminative way. It is not yet the ultimate peak of the mystical life. The summit of sanctity and happiness is to meet God, be united to Him, and lose oneself in Him. This final phase of perfection is called the unitive way—when a soul is hidden in God. St. Paul summed up this truth of the spiritual life in a famous text: *Vita vestra est abscondita cum Christo in Deo:* "Your life is hidden with Christ in God."[1]

Again, when our life is hidden in the soul of Christ, *cum Christo* (with Christ), we are in the illuminative way. When hidden with Christ in the profundities of the divinity—*in Deo* (in God)—we are in the unitive way. The Rosary, which throws open the illuminative way by leading us into the soul of the Savior, then initiates us into the secrets of the unitive way, enabling us to penetrate the innermost depths of the Divinity.

The Apostle St. John recalled with joy that his hands had touched the Word of Life: *Quod manus nostrae contrectaverunt de Verbo vitae:* "That which...our hands have handled of the Word of Life."[2] The Rosary brings us similar happiness, drawing us close to Christ Jesus, this Man whose name is honey in the mouth,

[1] Col. 3:3.
[2] 1 John 1:1.

music in the ear, and joy in the heart. Now, the divinity entirely permeates the Body of Christ. All the oil of the divinity poured forth upon the humanity of the Word through the hypostatic union, the ineffable unction that anointed Jesus. *Unixit te Deus oleo laetitae.*[3] *Unixit te Deus:* "Thy God hath anointed thee." His soul received this joyful anointing, His Heart and entire Being received it. This mysterious oil permeated every action of Our Redeemer. When His Heart sighed and His Soul trembled, it was God Who trembled.

To advance to the contemplation of the divinity, we need no other form of prayer than the Rosary. Suffice it to remember Whom each Mystery proposes for our consideration, Who is acting, and what action He performs. The Person is the Eternal Word. The action is theandric, that is to say, at the same time divine and human, and fully embalmed by the joyous unction of the Godhead. The Deity animates, quickens, and operates in every Mystery of the Rosary. Let us not dwell on the surface but delve into the very core of it. Its surface is the external events that form an essential part of the Mystery; its core is the interior of Jesus, His heart, soul, and divinity. Let us take refuge in these adorable abysses for a few moments, and perhaps we too will receive a little of that joyful unction that made Jesus the most beautiful of the sons of men.

Now that the Rosary has let us into the sanctuary of the divinity, it will help us to explore the depths of God. Is this cause for astonishment? Are the Mysteries of the Rosary not revealed to us by the almighty Spirit who, as St. Paul says, searches all things, and even the deep things of God: *Nobis autem revelavit Deus per Spirituum suum. Spiritus enim omnia scrutatur, etiam profunda Dei?*[4]

The profundities of God consist primarily in the intimate life of God Himself—the Eternal Family, the Adorable Trinity, the First Virgin. As St. Gregory of Nazianzus says, the First Beauty and the First Love: Three Divine Persons united in an

---

3   Ps. 44:8. "Thou hast loved justice, and hated iniquity: therefore God, thy God, hath anointed thee with the oil of gladness above thy fellows."

4   1 Cor. 2:10. "But to us God hath revealed them, by his Spirit. For the Spirit searcheth all things, yea, the deep things of God."

eternal embrace and unceasingly echoing to one another: love! love! love! This triple embrace is but a single embrace, and this triple love is but one love. *Et hi tres unum sunt*: "And these three are one."[5]

Now then, we find the Blessed Trinity in every Mystery of the Rosary. The three Persons are there because of the ineffable law that unites them to one another. While the Word alone assumed our frail human nature, all three cooperated in the Incarnation and Redemption. In the first Mystery, they hold counsel anew and repeat their creative word: "Let us make man to our image and likeness." When the great work is accomplished, and they see virginal Humanity coming forth from their hands, they say without irony, *Ecce Adam quasi unus ex nobis foetus est*: "Behold Adam is become as one of us."[6] Contemplating His innocent Humanity agonizing on the Cross, they pronounce the words of pardon: *Non igitur ultra percutiam omnem animam viventem sicut feci*: "Therefore, we will no more destroy every living soul as we have done."[7]

We have gone into the intimate life and counsels of the Trinity; let us now continue to scrutinize the divine abysses. Under another aspect, the deep things of God are His mercy and justice. How can we reconcile these two attributes: God's infinite vengeance upon sin and His infinite mercy toward the sinner? The Rosary gives us the key to this mystery. Suffice it to look upon the Cross in the fifth Sorrowful Mystery, where mercy and justice kiss in an eternal embrace.

At times, human justice falters shamelessly, faced with hypocritical entreaties or tears. Divine justice, however, never fails. When He forgives, God is just because Jesus made reparation for the guilty. Infinite love, infinite justice! Behold what God wrote on the Cross with the Blood of His Son. Let us also go up on the Cross, that we may embrace the divinity.

The mysteries of predestination and glory also give us some idea of the deep things of God. While the Rosary does not show these depths, at least it casts some consoling rays of light upon

---

[5] 1 John 5:7.
[6] Gen. 3:22.
[7] Gen. 8:21.

the darkness. It shows us Jesus the Model of all predestined and teaches us that we must be made conformable to this heavenly ideal: *quos prædestinavit conformes fieri imaginis Filii sui.*[8] The Glorious Mysteries of the Resurrection and Ascension give us a glimpse of eternal glory.

Eternity—yet another of the deep things of God—has already begun in us. The Rosary has the same power as the Faith because the Rosary summarizes the Faith in its most substantial core. Now, St. Bernard says that Faith has a span large enough to contain eternity itself. Through Faith and the Rosary, the future already exists in the present. St. Paul tells us that "Faith is the substance of things to be hoped for!" *Sperandarum substantia rerum.*[9] In other words, Faith is the immutable foundation that bears our immutable hopes.

St. Paul waxes even more emphatic: Faith, he says, is the beginning of God: *Initium substantiae ejus.*[10] The beginning of His substance. Therefore, through Faith and the Rosary, there is in the soul of a Christian a "seed" of God, the principle and beginning of eternity.

The Rosary brings us into contact with eternity because the Man-God whom we adore in each Mystery—to use the expression of St. Catherine of Siena—is the bridge between time and eternity. He touches time because of His human nature and eternity because of His divine nature and Person. As we start the recitation, we unite ourselves with the Man-God and allow ourselves to be carried over the bridge of infinity. As we end our prayer, we have unconsciously reached eternity. We thus have considered all the profundities of God revealed to us in the Rosary—the intimate life of the Blessed Trinity, divine mercy and justice, the mysteries of predestination and glory, eternity, and the secrets of the infinite.

Souls called to the spiritual union will find invaluable resources in the Rosary because it is the most sublime, surest,

---

8   Rom. 8:29. "For whom he foreknew, he also predestinated to be made conformable to the image of his Son; that he might be the firstborn amongst many brethren."

9   Heb. 11:1.

10 Heb. 3:14. "For we are made partakers of Christ: yet so, if we hold the beginning of his substance firm unto the end."

and easiest form of contemplation. It is the most sublime because it casts us into the depths of the infinite, where souls can meditate incessantly while never exhausting its riches. There are always new abysses to fathom. It is impossible to go beyond the divinity, and thus it is impossible to go farther or higher than the meditation of the Rosary.

It is the surest way. We risk deceiving ourselves if we consider divinity as living in the abstract, a form of life unrelated to man. The Rosary shows us the actual life of God and His dealings with man, making it His delight to dwell among us and converse with the children of men.

It is the easiest way. Our natural way of understanding is to rise from the material to the spiritual, from things visible to things invisible. When meditating on the Rosary, we rise from the visible humanity of the Word to the contemplation of the invisible divinity. We need no strenuous effort as we move smoothly and gradually from Christ visible to Christ God. The Son of Mary is God Himself. We can repeat the words of the Psalmist: *Quam bonus Israel Deus!* "How good is God to Israel!"[11]

We have only scratched the surface of all these beauties. Pious souls will know how to complete this study and savor these spiritual delicacies. They will also realize that the Rosary can meet everyone's needs.

There are souls not attracted to things invisible. Even when speaking to God, they feel the need to address a beating and throbbing heart of flesh like their own. In the Rosary, they will find the Heart of Jesus. Other souls are keenly intelligent and feed on spiritual beauties. Their penetrating eyes long to contemplate the heaven of spirits. They will find in the Rosary the soul of Jesus. Others soar toward the highest peaks of contemplation and can fix their gaze on the heaven of heavens. In the Rosary, they will find the divinity of Jesus. In short, you have the Sacred Heart for beginners, the soul of the Word for the more advanced, and divinity for the perfect.

However, these three states are never entirely separate. Even

---

[11] Ps. 72:1.

beginners must penetrate the soul and divinity of Jesus; the perfect must ever be mindful of His soul and heart. Heart, soul, and divinity are three abodes in which we must dwell at once: *trio tabernacula* (three abodes).[12] Oh, how delightful these three mansions are! These three eternal tabernacles are the beginning of heaven: Holiness.

Death will not separate us from this triple sojourn. On the contrary, it will enable us to dwell more perfectly in the heart, soul, and divinity of our Beloved. *Videbimus, laudabimus, amabimus*—"We shall see, praise, and love Him": unclouded vision, uninterrupted praise, undivided and integral love.

This wonderful trilogy of happiness begins right here with the Rosary. With you, O Mary, we shall ever abide in these three eternal tabernacles of your Son's heart, soul, and divinity, to praise and adore Him.

---

[12] Mark 9:4.

Part Two

Mary and Joseph, Models of Holiness

Carved sculpture of the Holy Family—Jesus, Mary and Joseph—in the Church of San Miguel de los Navarros in Zaragoza, Spain.

Chapter One

The Rosary and the Blessed Virgin Mary, Model of Predestination

Having tasted these supernatural delights at their source, after considering the Heart, Soul, and Divinity of Jesus in the Rosary, it is proper and desirable to consider the Queen of the Rosary herself. Before He died, Jesus Christ left us a twofold testament: The Eucharist and His Mother. Mary and the Eucharist! A priestly heart fills with joy at the very mention of these names as they sum up his interior peace and happiness. A virgin's heart rejoices, as from these two names, she draws all the austere delights of virginity. Jesus and Mary are the consolation and hope of the dying and promise forgiveness to sinners.

Mary and the Eucharist are also meaningful because they were the last parting gifts of Jesus to us. He instituted the Eucharist on the eve of His death and gave us His Mother shortly before He breathed His last. When a dying person leaves some gift, no matter how small, all those he leaves behind cherish it enormously. What happens when He who is dying is God? Here one's heart is touched to its innermost folds, and men have always realized the inestimable value of Jesus' last parting gifts to us. Mary and the Eucharist are the testaments of a dying God! No testament is or will be more hallowed than that. People have always had a passionate love for Mary and the Eucharist. Mary will be loved for as long as human hearts beat on this earth.

Therefore, devotion to the Blessed Virgin is a fundamental and indestructible part of Christianity, and the Rosary is the true expression of this devotion. For starters, it is the most powerful prayer we can address to Our Lady. We are like a baby whose repeated cries oblige his mother to come and help. A single Hail Mary already is a mighty cry for help. By repeating it ten times, we multiply its efficacy. When the entire decade is finished, we begin all over again until our canticle of love, repeated one hundred and fifty times, becomes a mighty cry that rises to heaven.

Secondly, when saying the Rosary, we assign to Mary her proper place in the divine plan. We go to God through Mary, do everything through Mary, expect all from Mary as if our salvation came through her. This is indeed Mary's role in the Incarnation; she truly is a cause of our salvation. To appreciate Our Lady's role in the Rosary properly, we must understand the role she played in the great work of Redemption.

When a masterpiece is broken and needs restoring, the artisan casts it a second time into the mold from which it came. Thus, the same mold serves to fix and fashion the handicraft. Man, a masterpiece of God, was crushed by the demon. To restore him to his perfection, God cast him once again into his original mold. That divine model is the Word of God, Who created and restored us through the Redemption. God decided to restore us through His Word, which is why He was made flesh. Hence, no one can obtain salvation except through Jesus Christ. To gain entrance into heaven, we must resemble our eternal exemplar. For us, predestination means to be made conformable to the image of the Son of God: *Praedestinavit conformes fieri imaginis Filii sui:*[1] Jesus is the mold of all predestined.

We can only be in awe as we remember these words of St. Augustine: Mary is the mold of Jesus. Indeed, there is an ineffable resemblance between the Body of Jesus and that of Mary, the Soul of Jesus and the soul of Mary, the predestination of Jesus and the predestination of Mary. The same act decreed the Incarnation and the existence of the Blessed Virgin. In the mind of God, the image of Christ and that of Mary were eternally united. Mary was indeed made to the likeness of Jesus and Jesus to her likeness. St. Augustine rightly called Mary

---

[1] Rom. 8:29. "For whom he foreknew, he also predestinated to be made conformable to the image of his Son; that he might be the firstborn amongst many brethren."

Formam Dei (the mold of God). Mary is the mold of Christ and thus the mold of God. Since it was in the designs of the Eternal Father that the first of His elect, head of all predestined, should be formed by the cooperation of the Blessed Virgin, all other saints must also be cast into that same virginal mold. As they come forth from it, they are other Christs, well-beloved and chosen ones. Just as God predestined us all to be made conformable to the image of His Son, so also He predestined us to be made conformable to the image of Mary.

How marvelous it is to consider that God created us to the likeness of Mary! He fashioned us after her so that we have some of her traits and beauty.

We are all fashioned in our Mother's mold whether called to the sublime summits of priesthood or secular professions. God contemplates Mary in the predestination of Christian spouses, mothers, virgins, religious, or priests.

When God forms the heart of a Christian spouse, He models it on the heart of Mary. He wants family life sanctified by a little of that chaste love that Mary had for St. Joseph. Mary's heart is the ideal model, after which God conceives the superb masterpiece that is the maternal heart. If we could contemplate the heroic love of every mother that ever existed, we should have a vast treasure; but all that love would be only a faint reflection of the heroism of the Mother of God. May mothers strive to live up to their sublime vocation! The more heroic they are, the closer they approach their heavenly ideal, predestined as they are to reflect the image of Mary.

The adorable Trinity is the ultimate model of virginity. In Mary, the Trinity contemplates Itself. Now, when predestinating virgins, God wants to model them after Mary. The Church has the utmost respect for her virgins and prescribes a solemn ceremony for consecrating a spouse of Christ—as if virtue alone were not enough to set them apart from the rest of humanity. Because of her state, the Church has for a virgin the same respect and reverence it has for the chalice of the altar. It consecrates a man or woman religious just as it consecrates a chalice.

Yet God treats His virgins with even greater respect by putting into their souls something radiant and angelic whose sight makes everyone look up to heaven. In short, He wants them to be the image and likeness of Mary on earth. Under the protection of their purity, they will go around the world, and people will stand in their presence as if they were in Mary's presence. Members of this chaste and immaculate generation are still numerous. They are ready to alleviate all suffering and misery, spiritual and temporal. They teach the ignorant, comfort the sick, sweeten the bitterness of frustrated hopes. Oh, virgins, be proud of your vocation! You have been fashioned in Mary's mold and destined to reflect her image in time and eternity.

Finally, God contemplates Mary when predestinating a priest. There is a striking analogy between Mary and a priest. Both are mediators between God and man. Mary is co-Redemptrix; the priest is co-redeemer. Because of his sacred ministry, he redeems souls by raising them from the death of sin and restoring them to grace through the Sacraments. Since both Mary and the priest are virgins, both can say to Jesus, though in a different sense, *Filius meus es tu, ego hodie genui te:* "Thou art my son, this day have I begotten thee." [2] When the priest consecrates the host, Jesus is born again in that sacramental and mysterious existence that He leads on our altars.

Oh, divine enjoyment! Oh, inexpressible sweetness! Mary and the priest meet in the same happiness, in the same word: *Filius meus es tu:* "O Jesus, you are my God and my Son!" Mary and the priest also engender Jesus in souls: Mary uses the priest to give life to the sinner, and the priest needs Mary to act effectively. Our vocation is thus similar to that of Mary. Thank you, my God, for forming us on the model of Your Mother. Thank you for having predestined us to become conformed to her: *Praedestinavit conformes fieri.*

Such is the role of the Blessed Virgin Mary in the mystery of predestination: Spouses, virgins, and priests are all cast into this immaculate mold. Now, eternal predestination is fulfilled in time only with man's free cooperation. With God's help through the intercession of Mary, we must realize the divine ideal with our own efforts to reproduce her model faithfully.

---

[2]   Ps. 2:7.

To that end, we must have that model always before our eyes. Mary poses before us in the Rosary, as it were; each Mystery reveals one of her traits.

All that we have said about the Heart and Soul of Jesus equally applies to Mary. The Mysteries manifest to us the heart and soul of Mary with all their treasures and inexpressible beauties. That makes it easy for us to imitate this perfect predestination model by practicing the virtue contemplated in each Mystery. For example, we could devote one week to cultivating the virtue of humility as seen in Mary, another week to charity, and so on. If one week does not suffice, let us devote months or years, but let us make sure to shape our souls according to our model. Once Mary's traits are "etched" in our souls, may we never allow them to be effaced by negligence but always contemplate our Mother's beloved image in us.

The Virgin and Christ Child Giving a Rosary to
Saint Dominic, Mexico.

Chapter Two

The Rosary and the Blessed Virgin Mary, Mother of Grace

We have seen how the Rosary makes us conformable to the Immaculate Mother of Jesus—the marvelous ideal of our predestination. Since predestination in our souls takes place through the action of grace, let us examine the role the Blessed Virgin plays concerning grace.

Since grace is a participation in the divine nature, God alone can produce it in us, as He alone can communicate His own life and nature to us. As God, Jesus is like His Father, the Author of grace. As God and Man, He is the leading meritorious cause of all spiritual goods. Furthermore, His Adorable Humanity possesses a profound and mysterious efficacy in that It is the instrument that God employs daily to produce grace in us. The Gospel tells us that power went forth from Our Lord that healed people's bodies. The Humanity of the Word is the perfumed atmosphere where the drops of divine dew form: from It escapes a powerful virtue that heals our souls by pouring sanctifying grace into them.

If Jesus Christ is the sole reservoir of the fertile waters of salvation, Mary is the channel through which they come to us. While she is not the source, as she too received everything from her Son, everything must pass through her to reach us. Of herself, she does not produce grace, as grace is participation from God. Now, God willed to make Our Lady the dispenser of all graces. In order to come to us, the divine waves of the vast Ocean, which is Christ, flow through the virginal river, which is Mary. Hence that famous saying of St. Bernard: *Nulla gratia venit de caelo ad terram nisi transeat per manus Mariae:* "No grace comes from heaven to earth without passing through the hands of Mary." The holy Doctors and Fathers of the Church cannot find enough words to teach this truth. They speak of Mary as the reservoir of all goods: *promptuarium omnium bonorum*— the treasurer of all graces of Jesus Christ. Even before them, the Archangel St. Gabriel had summed it up in one word: *Gratia plena*. She is full of grace for both herself and us: *Plena sibi, superplena nobis*.

St. Thomas distinguishes a triple fullness of grace.[1] First, *plenitudo sufficientiae*: the fullness of sufficiency common to all the just. That means that all the elect receive an abundance of grace, sufficient to enable them to observe the divine law and lead them to eternal bliss.

Secondly, there is *plenitudo excellentiae*, the fullness of excellence. It belongs to Christ alone, who possesses the fullness of the source, the plenitude of a boundless abyss. From Him come all our riches. *De plenitudine ejus nos omnes accepimus:* "Of His fullness we all have received."[2]

Lastly, there is *plenitudo redundantiae*, the fullness of superabundance. It belongs to the Blessed Virgin Mary especially, for the grace she received is like a reservoir that overflows and floods all humanity. Mary is full of grace for herself and super abounds with grace for us—*Plena sibi, superplena nobis*. Of her, we can say, as we say of her Son, though in a different sense: *De plenitudine ejus nos omnes accepimus*—"Of His fullness we all have received."[3]

The graces of the Blessed Virgin have a threefold value: meritorious value, satisfactory value, and impetrative value. According to several holy Doctors, her merits surpass those of the angels and men combined, as satisfaction and impetration go hand in hand with merit.

Our august Mother's spiritual treasures attain heights and depths that are impossible to comprehend. Thus, it is not astonishing that they would overflow and pour into our souls:

---

[1]   See his commentary on the Hail Mary and the one on John 1:10.

[2]   John 1:16.

[3]   Idem.

plenitudo redundantiae (the fullness of superabundance). Her satisfactory treasures are entirely at our disposal. Having been exempt from the slightest stain of sin, she needs not to atone for herself. Thus, her satisfactions are placed in the treasury of the Church, which distributes them to us through indulgences. Her merits do not apply directly to us because they are her inalienable property. However, we can say that Mary is a meritorious cause of grace—not that she merited salvation for us in strict justice like Jesus. But she has an extraordinary power to move the heart of God because of her close friendship with Him. Mary is the dispenser of all graces especially through impetration, meaning that all our spiritual goods come only through her intercession. Therefore, the words of St. Bernard are not a pious exaggeration, but express a beautiful truth that is worthwhile to study in-depth.

Here we must recall the sublime teaching that St. Paul expounded in such a magnificent fashion.[4] He declares that the Church is a mystical body of which Christ is the Head. As in the human body, in the Church, there are powerful nerves that maintain her different members in unity, nerves signified by spiritual authority. Then there are vessels that support life, namely the Sacraments. Finally, there is grace, which is the Church's life and blood. All movement and energy descend from the head to the members. Just as a human body has a neck that unites the head with the rest of the body, so Christ is the Head of the Church, and Mary is the neck that connects the head with the members: *Maria, collum Ecclesiae!* Mary is the mystical neck of the divine body, which is the Church.

Just as all movements and energies reach the rest of the body from the head only by going through the neck, so also the life of Christ reaches the faithful only by passing through Mary. This supernatural organ connects the mystical Head with members of the body. Grace descends from Christ to the Blessed Virgin, from whom it descends into our souls. From our souls, it again rises to eternity, from whence it came. Grace, like blood and water, seeks its source. The source of grace is eternity, and grace

---

4   Eph. 4:16.

mysteriously flows back to eternity, according to the words of Our Lord: *Fiat in eo fons aquae salientis in vitam aeternam:*[5] "In him, it will become a fountain of water, springing up into life everlasting."

Grace flows back into eternity in the same way it came. From the soul, it rises to Mary; from Mary, it passes into Christ and through Christ, it finally reaches eternity again. Thus, there is in the Church a supernatural stream perpetually rising and descending through Mary as an ebb and flow between heaven and earth. The heart of Mary transmits to us the merits and treasures of Jesus; our merits and love reach Jesus through the heart of His Mother. Your heart, O Immaculate Mother, is the sweet rendezvous where God and man meet—the mysterious river that joins the banks of time and eternity.

The waves of this grace seem to raise their sublime voices, more admirable than the great oceans, crying out with eternal echoes: *Maria, Mater gratiae:* "Mary, Mother of grace!" May we unite the harmony of our hearts with this harmony in praising God!

Such is the role of Mary in the economy of salvation. Now the Rosary is an excellent means to tap into this channel of grace. As the Sacraments apply to us the treasures of Jesus Christ, keeping all proportions and without any exaggeration, so the Rosary applies to us the treasures of Mary. Where else will we find the merits and satisfaction of the Blessed Virgin? Is the Rosary not the story of her life?

In the Mysteries, her satisfaction and merits multiply almost to infinity. The same happens to her prayer's impetrative power. She intercedes for us and asks her Son to grant our petition based on her role in the events contemplated in the fifteen Mysteries of the Rosary. Thus, by meditating on the Rosary, we encounter the source from which Mary drew her spiritual riches. As we said when speaking about the soul of Jesus, the Rosary puts us in touch with the soul and grace of the Blessed Virgin, and her soul sends off rays of light that enlighten our soul. When we recite the Hail Mary and say *gratia plena*, we

---

[5] 1 John 4:14.

not only recall her early joys, but also remember her role in the work of salvation and the economy of grace and her powerful influence with God on our behalf. To meditate on the Mysteries is to keep our heart and soul united to hers and quench our thirst at the same fountain; it is to join our voices in time and eternity to say, "O Mary, Mother of grace, remember your children!" To this prayer, she graciously replies, "He that shall find me shall find life and shall have salvation from the Lord."[6]

A statue of Our Lady as described in the Apocalypse graces the main square's column in Maribor, Slovenia, in thanksgiving for the end of the plague of 1680.

Chapter Three

The Rosary and the Blessed Virgin Mary, Patroness of a Good Death

There are, in the life of every Christian, three unique events that solemnly reverberate in eternity: his baptism, his first communion, and his death. The day of our baptism is the beginning of bright days, when God takes possession of our soul, marking us with His seal as His own, and anoints us kings for eternity. Our first communion is a feast in heaven and on earth. It is the ineffable moment when a child can embrace his long-absent father, but even more so as a child embraces his God for the first time. It is at our first communion that we kiss Jesus in the Eucharist for the first time. However, the most solemn and decisive day of all certainly is the day of our death, in which either we triumph or plunge into utter despair. It is the day that changes us and forever seals our blessed predestination or eternal doom.

These three crucial days are placed under Mary's blessing. She smiles on us at our birth and holds us in her arms, as it were, at our baptism. She blesses us at our first communion and leads us to the banquet of her Son. Above all, she blesses and smiles at us on the day of our death. Holy Scripture calls death the day of the Lord, *dies Domini*. We could also call it the day of Mary.

It has to be so.

A dying sinner faces three awful scenarios. He sees his past life with all its sins, his horrible future, and the avenging flames that await him. He sees the present and the divine justice from which he cannot escape. His judgment begins on his deathbed.

Theologians believe that man is judged in the exact spot where he dies. Oh, how dreadful it would be if the day of death were the day of strict divine justice! Yet, it is also Mary's day, and hence it is a day of mercy and joy. In the face of those three gloomy scenarios, Mary places before the eyes of the dying three ineffably consoling visions. The person has a sweet vision of his past and all the favors that she gave him. He sees Paradise, the eternal kingdom where she reigns as Queen. He sees divine mercy, protection, and even—as has often occurred—also her presence and smile. No matter what temptations assail the child of Mary, his heavenly Mother strengthens and consoles him.

O pious children of the heavenly Queen, we do not have to fear death because it is Mary's day! Our august Mother deserves the title of the patroness of a happy death above all in two ways. She prevents death from surprising us and helps us in a special way in our dreadful passage.

Dying in the state of grace is a favor we cannot merit. Only God, absolute Master of grace and death, can unite death and the state of grace. Thus, the death of the just is a favor from heaven and shows special predestination. The same love of God that gives us life also causes our death. The same act that calls us to glory decrees that we die at that moment. By some coincidence, a child just baptized can fall from his mother's arms and die. To us this may appear fortuitous; but in God's designs, it is a special grace by which that child is predestined to die at that moment.

To obtain the grace of final perseverance for her children, Mary has given countless acts of kindness that escape us. Sometimes, dying a year, month, week, day, or moment earlier is an inestimable favor that she does us without our knowledge. She chooses a moment when we are in the state of grace. As for the reprobates, God strikes them at random. They are the deadwood destined for the eternal fires. But, as a pious author put it, for the servants of Mary, who are the fragrant wood of the garden of delights, He observes the seasons. While death can come suddenly, it does not surprise them, as premonition or inner voice warns them. Even when their death seems unforeseen, in hindsight, we realize that in their last days, these souls were more fervent, more recollected, and more united to Our Lord.

Secondly, at the terrible moment of death, Mary aids her children in an exceptional way. As St. Alphonsus writes, by assisting at Calvary at the death of the Head of the predestined, Mary obtained the privilege of assisting all other predestined souls in their last agony. Just as God decreed that His Christ should become flesh through Mary and die before her eyes, He also decreed that His other 'Christs' be formed by Mary and that she would receive their last sigh.

The last moments of a predestined soul are solemn indeed. A kind of stupor permeates the bystanders. In awe, they feel that God is there and keep silent. However, God is not alone with the soul. The devil and his henchmen are there too. Realizing that his time is running out, Satan makes a final onslaught to grab his victim. Wait! Mary arrives! More terrible than an army in battle array, she strikes down the infernal giant with a single look. As St. Antoninus says, if Mary is for us, who is against us?

St. Alphonsus assures us that Mary has been seen assisting at the deathbed of her faithful servants, wiping the sweat of agony off their faces and refreshing their fevered brows. She is there to make sure that death becomes a drink they taste with delight. At times, one even hears holy souls, like the pious Suarez and a saintly Dominican nun, crying out: "Ah! I never knew it was so sweet to die!"

Mary tenderly lulls her children to sleep like a loving mother; her beloved die in the embrace of the Lord, savoring both that embrace and the inebriation of death. When St. Clare was about to breathe her last, the Blessed Virgin appeared by her deathbed with a group of virgins. She lovingly embraced the dying saint and gave her a kiss of peace as the virgins surrounded that triumphal bed with a golden cloth.

It is a custom in the order of St. Dominic to sing the *Salve Regina* at the deathbed of a member. More than once, during the singing of this beautiful antiphon, the dying religious suddenly smiled sweetly and then slept peacefully in the Lord, as if cradled in the arms of Mary.

We do not know what kind of death God has reserved for us. We do know, however, that if we continue as faithful servants of Mary to the end, we will be consoled in our last moment. However bitter that hour might be, our Mother will sweeten it for us. We will savor death as a delicious beverage prepared by the hands of our Mother, and our last day will be a beautiful day of Mary.

With these thoughts, we have not strayed from considering the Rosary. In its Mysteries, Mary begins her office as patroness of a happy death. First, she assists St. Joseph, her glorious spouse, in his agony. Later on, at the fifth Sorrowful Mystery, she assists the King of the Elect. While the Master of life assuredly needed no assistance to die, He wished the presence of His tender Mother to assuage the bitterness of His cruel sacrifice. The Rosary reminds us of three ineffable deaths: the deaths of Jesus, Mary, and Joseph.

The Mystery of the Agony of Jesus gives us divine strength to overcome the demon's attacks as our agony approaches. When meditating on the Mysteries of the Crucifixion and Assumption, we can unite our souls to dying Jesus and moribund Mary so that through their deaths, the King and Queen of the elect grant us special graces when our own time comes. It is in this school that one learns how to die. When death arrives, a Rosary Knight looks it in the face like a worker who knows his trade. Anyone who has meditated well on the Crucifixion and the Assumption knows the harsh and sweet craft of death. When saying these Mysteries, let us not forget to ask for the grace of final perseverance to attain that great end, as they are particularly associated with a happy death.

We can also say that each of the fifteen Mysteries and each Hail Mary will obtain for us this supreme grace, as each time we beg Our Lady: "Pray for us now and at the hour of our death," we are asking for a public and solemn rendezvous at our last agony. Mary will not fail to come to our aid. She will rescue the members of her honor guard and obtain a pardon for their sins if needed.

The Rosary is the school wherein we can learn to die well; whoever is faithful to it will be able to look death fearlessly in the face.

Several trustworthy authors report on this episode in the life of St. Dominic. Through the saint's efforts, a young woman enrolled herself in the Confraternity of the Rosary. Shortly afterward, she died suddenly, and her body was thrown into a well. Having heard the tragic news, Dominic hastened to the edge of the well and, in a loud voice, called the dead woman by name. She came forth alive, confessed her sins with tears and contrition, and lived for another two days. She said that she would undoubtedly have been damned if the merits of the Rosary had not obtained for her the grace of perfect contrition.

This story helps us understand how Our Lady exercises through the Rosary her office as the patroness of a happy death. The glories of Mary and the glories of the Rosary are inseparable.

We have said that one can sum up the issue of salvation in three words: predestination, grace, and death. Likewise, three words can summarize the role Mary plays in it. She is the model of the predestined, the Mediatrix of all grace, and the patroness of a happy death. For its part, the Rosary helps us to imitate the model of our predestination, communicates to us the graces that God gives us through the hands of the Blessed Mother, and obtains for us the grace of a happy death.

Through the Rosary, we assign to Our Lady her proper place in the divine plan. Despite the claims of sixteenth-century innovators and rationalists of later times, the Rosary is a fundamental devotion of Christianity and a sure means of sanctification.

Saint Joseph, foster-father of Our Lord.
Saint Joseph's Church, Nazareth, Israel

Chapter Four

The Rosary and Saint Joseph

The Holy Spirit inscribed three names on the first page of the Gospel, frequently chanted by the ministers of the Church at her altars. *Cum esset desponsata mater Jesu, Maria, Joseph*: "When Mary, the Mother of Jesus, was espoused to Joseph." These three names—Jesus, Mary, Joseph—are inseparably united and repeated continuously until the end of time. God has written them in the book of life so that we inscribe them in our hearts and affections.

In the Mysteries of the Rosary, the remembrance of Joseph is inseparable from that of Jesus and Mary. The Rosary reveals not only Mary and her Son but also St. Joseph, her spouse. The Rosary can be called the life story of Joseph, as it helps us, first, to see the role the Holy Patriarch played in the Incarnation and Redemption, and, second, his position concerning the Church. We will now meditate on this twofold point of view.

A Virgin Trinity created the world; a Virgin Trinity redeemed the world. We invoke the Virgin Trinity that created us at the beginning of our actions—Father, Son, and Holy Spirit. The Virgin Trinity that redeemed the world is Jesus, Mary, and Joseph, whose names we have learned to know and love from our childhood. In this Trinity of salvation, Jesus is the Redeemer, Mary is Mother of the Redeemer, and Joseph is united to both by ineffable bonds. All three are virgins and form a single family with shared joys and sufferings. Of them, we can say what we say of the heavenly Trinity, though in a different sense: *Et hi tres unum sunt*—and these three are one.

United to Jesus and Mary by sacred bonds, Joseph had real rights over them. A wife belongs to her husband. Between them, there is a total mutual donation. In the case of Mary and Joseph, their union was spiritual, and hence it was an even stronger and perfect union—one virginity espousing another virginity. Mary belonged entirely to Joseph.

Consequently, Jesus became the property of Mary's spouse, Joseph. St. Francis de Sales has a very ingenious comparison that we borrow to illustrate this point. If a bird drops fruit into a garden, the tree springing up from the seed without any doubt belongs to the garden's owner. Mary was the garden of St. Joseph, wherein the Holy Spirit placed the divine fruit, which became a great tree that healed and sheltered the entire human race. Oh, rich and blessed Patriarch, owner of the two marvels of grace!

When creating Jesus and Mary, as the prophet says, the Almighty had to move heaven and earth: *Commovebo caelum et terram*.[1] Eternity somehow roused to accomplish this great marvel, which has been called *negotium saeculorum*, the task of the ages. After having shaken the universe and made His two masterpieces, God decided to give them to St. Joseph, who thus received the most beautiful creations. Henceforth, Joseph could say of Jesus and Mary: "You are mine," and both could answer, "Yes, we are."

To be worthy of possessing the Lord's two greatest treasures, being the husband of Mary and foster-father of her child, St. Joseph had to be endowed with a super-eminent grace that would take him to the very apex of heroic holiness. Echoing ancient teaching, St. John Chrysostom asserts that Joseph was cleansed from all stains of original sin before his birth. Later, his daily contact with the Word Incarnate must undoubtedly have led to an unfathomable increase of grace in his soul.

Let us recall a principle of St. Thomas we have often referred to here: the closer something is to a source, the more abundantly it shares the properties of that source. Who, other than Mary, came into closer contact with the Humanity of the Word than

---

[1] Aggeus 2:7. "For thus saith the Lord of hosts: Yet one little while, and I will move the heaven and the earth, and the sea, and the dry land."

Joseph? As he held Jesus in his arms and kissed Him, was he not drinking from the very source of holiness? The Humanity of Christ, the ocean of grace, poured grace over his soul and filled it even to overflowing. The Incarnation comprises three unfathomable mysteries: the grace bestowed on Jesus, Mary, and Joseph, which we will only know well in our marvelous contemplation in eternity.

Furthermore, the mere presence of Mary would have sufficed to sanctify her spouse.

Let us borrow a comparison from St. Francis de Sales. Suppose a mirror directly receives the sun's rays as another mirror is placed right in front of it. While this second mirror receives the sunrays only by reflection, they nonetheless are perfectly reflected. Mary is the mirror that receives the rays of the sun of justice directly. Joseph is the mirror that receives those rays from Mary. Thus, Joseph's soul reflects the splendors of Christ and Mary, which explains his incomparable holiness. That is how St. Joseph associates to the Redeemer and His Mother in the work of salvation as part of the virginal and redemptive trinity of Nazareth.

The Joyful Mysteries admirably reveal to us St. Joseph's role in the Incarnation as the spouse of Mary and foster-father of Jesus. The Annunciation and Visitation acquaint us with him as the spouse of the Immaculate Virgin. The Nativity, Purification, and Meeting at the Temple show him especially as the foster-father of Jesus. Pious meditation on this Mystery unveils to us some graces and feelings radiating from the glorious Patriarch's soul. In fact, the seven joys and seven sorrows summarize his entire life story. The first part of the Rosary is a living account of this interior drama of suffering and joys, while the Joyful Mysteries are like a limpid surface that reflects the serene sky of Joseph's soul.

Is the remembrance of the Holy Patriarch absent from the Sorrowful Mysteries? After Our Lord's Crucifixion, the Soul of the Word descended into Limbo. What an incomparable scene, the souls of Jesus and Joseph together once again! St. Thomas teaches that in Limbo, our Redeemer bestowed the beatific vision on the souls of the just. What a happy moment they experienced as they beheld God face-to-face! Imagining St. Joseph's joy at that point, let us ask his intercession so that one day we may join him in eternal bliss.

As we delve into the Glorious Mysteries, we again meet our beloved patron, who undoubtedly was among the privileged souls that escorted the Soul of Christ on the morning of the Resurrection. The triumph of Jesus is also the triumph of Joseph. The foster-father rose gloriously with his Son on Ascension Thursday. Now, as our Savior sits at the right hand of the Almighty as King and Judge, He makes St. Joseph sit next to Him and entrusts His Church to him to whose care He was confided during His earthly life.

As we congratulate our Savior on His triumphal entrance into heaven, we congratulate St. Joseph for sharing His Empire. In the last Mysteries, as we meditate on the glories of Mary, we may recall the Venerable Patriarch's role in them. Mary will be grateful to us for joining in the same meditation of her husband's triumphs with her own. As we pray to the Queen of the Church, we pay homage to St. Joseph, patron and protector of the Church.

Thus, the Glorious Mysteries reveal the influence that St. Joseph exercises over the universal Church.

The Church was established primarily to perpetuate the Incarnation through the ages. The Incarnation and the Church are the summits of the world's history. The Church is the necessary prolongation of the Incarnation. The Christian family is the continuation of the family of Nazareth. Therefore, St. Joseph should play in the Church a role similar to the one he had in the Incarnation. He must exert upon the Christian family a role analogous to the one he played in the Family of Nazareth as its guardian and protector. He is now the guardian and protector of Christendom.

The Church has solemnly recognized this role the holy Patriarch plays in her regard. Let us recall that a Dominican religious, Fr. Lataste, offered his life to have St. Joseph declared patron of the Church. His generous sacrifice was accepted. Shortly after his death, Pius IX issued a decree proclaiming St. Joseph patron of the universal Church.

Thus, St. Joseph's role is to be the Patron of the Universal Church. That means that as our intercessor, he can obtain for us every grace whatever our station in life may be.

We all know St. Teresa of Avila's famous saying: The Almighty grants His saints favors only to help us in particular cases. However, I know from experience that the glorious St. Joseph has the power to help everyone. We have shown how all our spiritual goods come through Jesus and Mary. Jesus is the fountain of grace, and Mary is the channel through which it flows. Now, Joseph has property rights over the two. In heaven, the bonds that united the Holy Family on earth have been enshrined rather than destroyed. In paradise, as he did on earth, St. Joseph may say, "You are mine," and both can still answer: "Yes, we are." In a sense, therefore, St. Joseph can command them. Yet, Jesus and Mary do not wait for him to ask. They anticipate his wishes and immediately grant all the favors he wants for his privileged children.

Given his influence with the King and Queen of Heaven, Joseph may be called the minister of spiritual treasures, treasurer of divine finances, and distributor of God's spiritual and temporal graces. A female religious congregation in the United States needed a considerable sum of money to build an establishment to help the poor. The nuns invoked St. Joseph's intercession, and one of them composed a hymn to honor him. Every evening, after night prayers, the elderly would sing that moving song. At the end of the novena, a benefactor sent them a generous sum of money. Filled with greater confidence, the elderly continued praying until St. Joseph graciously obtained for them double the sum required.

Do we want to solve a difficult case? Let us turn to the one who is the advocate of desperate causes. When a Christian family threatened with an unjust lawsuit was making a novena to St. Joseph, the plaintiff himself came forward and offered to stop the proceedings and pay for the costs.

Yet, Joseph shows himself to be our powerful intercessor, especially in spiritual matters. How many grateful Christian mothers come to his altar to thank him for converting a son or husband?

Undoubtedly, the supreme grace one can ask is final perseverance and a happy death. While unable to answer the sobering question of whether we will be saved or damned, St. Joseph, who gave up his soul in the arms of Jesus and Mary, will obtain this supreme grace for his devotees.

St. Vincent Ferrer often recounted this story. A pious merchant regularly invited three poor people to his table to honor the Holy Family of Nazareth once a year. As his last moments approached, Jesus, Mary, and Joseph appeared to him smiling and said, "During your life, you received us in your home every year. Today, we will receive you into our heavenly home." If only we could receive such an invitation during our agony! Let us at least make sure to ask St. Joseph the invaluable gift of final perseverance.

St. Joseph is, therefore, the intercessor for all graces and the patron of everyone in every condition. Having sheltered the Infant Jesus under his fatherly mantle, he is the patron of childhood. As head of the most illustrious Family of Nazareth that ever existed, he is the patron of all Christian families. He is especially the patron of workers. While belonging to the royal lineage of David, he is known to the faithful under a more modest yet revered name: the carpenter of Nazareth.

Espoused to a virgin mother and foster-father to a virgin God, he is undoubtedly the guardian of virginity. He is the patron of priests, as both Joseph and the priest have received the mission of taking Jesus to men and defending Him against His enemies, and the gift of being closely united to the Savior and living and dying on His Heart.

Joseph tasted the bitter cup of seven sorrows during his life and is thus the patron of the afflicted and suffering. Having been forced to flee his native country and taste how hard it is not to behold the sky of his motherland, He is the patron of exiles. Having worked as a carpenter, he is the patron saint of workers. No matter his condition or state in life, everyone can find in him a model, protector, and friend. As the universal patron of the Church, he is the patron of all Christians.

In short, this is the mission that Jesus Christ entrusted to His foster-father on Ascension Day, which shows us how meditation on the Rosary can truly become a meditation on St. Joseph.

Leo XIII rightly understood the connection between the head of the Holy Family and the Mysteries of the Rosary. Accordingly, he decreed that during the month of the Rosary, Joseph, the spouse of Mary, be invoked immediately after his Immaculate Spouse and a prayer in his honor be added at the end of the Rosary.

Let us not separate those whom God has united. From now on, when saying the Rosary, let us lovingly associate the Mother of Jesus with St. Joseph, her spouse.

Part Three

The Rosary and the
Practice of Holiness

*A familiar sight to millions of pilgrims from around the world:
the Rosary Basilica of Lourdes in the evening just before the
torchlight Rosary Procession.*

Chapter One

The Rosary, Source of Holiness

God wants us to be perfect even as He is perfect. God has not called us unto uncleanness but unto sanctification, says the Apostle. A Christian is a consecrated person, which means set apart. Indeed, an all-encompassing consecration extends through our entire existence like a divine network that embraces us entirely, so we are preserved from worldly contagion and always remain everywhere the property of the Lord.

Look at what the Church does to sanctify us. As we arrive in this world, she welcomes us in her arms, marks and consecrates us: it is her taking possession. At our baptism, she does upon us a mysterious anointing and pours a little water on our heads: we are saints! When our supreme agony draws near, she again impresses on us the seal of salvation by anointing us the last time with the Sacrament of Extreme Unction: We are consecrated and ready to die. After our death, she blesses even our dust in the tomb. Our remains thus keep a kind of majesty even in corruption, and God will remember that we were consecrated for resurrection and glory.

The Church blesses her children, especially when they must choose a state in life. She blesses her virgins to be more attracted to chastity, and have purer hearts as victims of love. She blesses her monks so they can more easily bear the royal burden of the religious vocation. She anoints and sanctifies her priests upon ordination so they can confidently go through the world. She blesses Christian spouses, so their union is lasting and happy and pours into their hearts a little of that charity with which

Christ cherishes His Church.

Our first holiness is the consecration, which marks all Christians whatever their state may be. It inscribes on our foreheads this motto, which many unfortunately respect so little: *Sanctum Domino*—"You are holy unto the Lord!"

That, however, is exterior holiness. Properly so called, holiness is a participation in the very being of God, a state of soul that unites us to Our Lord so intimately that we are quickened only by His life and love. A saint is one who can say, "And I live, now not I, but Christ lives in me."[1]

We will now try to show how the Rosary communicates to us that holiness which is the very life of God. In the human body, the head and heart are the two main organs that sustain life. The Church also has a head from which descends all supernatural energies and a heart that circulates these divine energies throughout the body. Jesus Christ is the Head of the Church, and the Holy Spirit is her heart.

St. Thomas says that Christ is called the Head of the Church by analogy with the human head. In a head, one can consider three things: order, because it is the first part of man beginning from the top; perfection, because all the senses, interior and exterior, dwell in the head whereas other members have only the sense of touch; power, because the energy, movement, and guidance of the other members come from the head's intellectual and driving power.

Now then, in the spiritual order, these three things belong to Christ. He ranks first because of His closeness to God. His grace is the highest, as all other men have received grace only because of it. Secondly, He has perfection. As St. John says, He had the fullness of all graces: "We saw Him full of grace and truth."[2] Finally, He has the power of bestowing grace on all members of the Church, as the same Evangelist writes, "And of his fullness, we all have received."[3]

Christ is like the head because of His visible humanity. Because of His inner and hidden role, the Holy Spirit is like

---

[1]   Gal. 2:20.
[2]   John 1:14.
[3]   John 1:16.

the heart. In a secret and mysterious operation, the Paraclete invisibly vivifies and unifies the Church. He maintains her life, ardor, beauty, and perpetual youth. He consoles and fortifies her. He is like a torrential river that makes the city of God fertile and happy. He is the mysterious yet all-powerful heart that casts forth life and grace.

Such, therefore, is the economy of the supernatural life: to advance in perfection and obtain salvation, we must be united to both head and heart, Christ and the Holy Spirit.

Now then, meditating on the Rosary smoothly unites us with both. Meditating on the fifteen Mysteries, we meet the adorable Person of Jesus Christ and consider His life, actions, and infinite virtue. We plunge into His Soul and Divinity. As our Divine Head, He communicates His life and movements to us to feel and say we now have a living soul: *Foetus est homo in animam viventem*: "Man has become a living soul."[4]

We can also perceive the operation of the Holy Spirit in each Mystery. He was the One Who had the Immaculate Virgin conceive, made John the Baptist leap in his mother's womb, and transformed Elizabeth and Zachary. He directed the whole course of the Passion of Jesus and finally animated the entire series of Glorious Mysteries.

The Holy Spirit is the power and heart of every Mystery. If we earnestly wish to delve into the depths of this devotion, the adorable Paraclete will, so to speak, become our own heart and pulsate so strongly as to lead our soul to eternal glory.

The Rosary clearly unites us with Christ and the Holy Spirit, the Head and Heart of the Church. Now, when in the company of the Son and the Paraclete, you are also in that of the Father. We are thus in the bosom of the most adorable Trinity, the very source of life, love, holiness, and happiness!

---

[4] Gen. 2:7.

Statue of "La Vierge Couronnée"—the Crowned Virgin—
in the Sanctuary of Our Lady of Lourdes, France.

Chapter Two

The Rosary and Common Holiness

To better appreciate how the Rosary influences our spiritual life, we should consider the three degrees of holiness—ordinary holiness, perfect holiness, and heroic holiness. Ordinary holiness consists of observing the commandments and precepts by a soul in the state of grace. It is that first degree of charity, that wedding garment without which we cannot attend the banquet of the Father.

No extraordinary or multiple actions are needed to attain this first degree in spiritual life. The Rosary offers clear examples for the simplest minds. During His life in Nazareth, Jesus Christ, our Model of holiness, did nothing but ordinary actions in an unpretentious way. Mary and Joseph, our next models in the way of perfection, led a hidden and obscure life whose divine fabric was made of small actions. Holiness does not consist in accomplishing extraordinary deeds. Since working and suffering is the common condition of humanity, holiness consists in knowing how to work and suffer.

The Rosary is the true school of labor and suffering.

What do we find as we meditate on the Joyful Mysteries and enter the little house at Nazareth? A workshop, a carpenter, and his helper—something almost unfathomable. The Son, born of the Father in the splendors of eternity, does not wish to reign on a throne or dwell in a palace but to become a simple artisan and be called a laborer. The Jews asked: *Nonne hic est fabri filius?*—"Is this not the carpenter's son?"[1] *Nonne hic est fabrius, filius Mariae?*—"Is this not the carpenter, Son of Mary?"[2]

Ah! If Christian workers would only learn from these great lessons, they would tell the rich of this world: I envy not your wealth as God Himself thought nothing of it but became a poor worker like me. If only employers and employees remembered the kind relationships between Jesus and Joseph, the social question would be swiftly solved, and peace and happiness would soon be restored to so many desolate households. If people practiced the lessons taught by the Rosary, every workshop would resemble the home of Nazareth. The joy of the Holy Family would enter every family, and the world could welcome a golden age, as holiness would reign overall.

The Sorrowful Mysteries will teach us how to sanctify our suffering. A person who properly meditates on the Rosary does not complain of his lot. You may feel exhausted and covered with sweat; but did you ever sweat blood like Jesus Christ? Your body may writhe in pain; were you ever submitted to vicious scourging? Your mind is troubled with concerns; did you ever have to wear a bloody crown of thorns? Was your head pierced with thorns, were your eyes filled with blood as those of Jesus? Your shoulders bend under heavy burdens; did you ever have to bear the heavy weight of a cross as Jesus on His way up to Golgotha? Your hands and feet are weary with work; were they ever pierced with terrible nails that crush every fiber and nerve? Your soul is full of anguish; did it ever plunge into the abyss of grief that drew this cry of agony from Our Redeemer: "My God, My God, why hast Thou forsaken me?" Oh, no! A soul who understands the Rosary dares not complain.

At times, we hear people saying, "I would not mind had I deserved this suffering!" Now, did Our Redeemer deserve His agony, His scourging and Crucifixion? We are lucky and blessed if we suffer undeservedly. A deserved trial is a punishment; undeserved suffering is a precious grace—God visiting and smiling at us.

We cannot gauge how seriously we hurt ourselves by rejecting

1   Matt. 13:55.
2   Mark 6:3.

the cross. Suffering, say the holy Doctors, has a threefold effect on the soul: it expiates, impetrates, and sanctifies. Nothing purifies the soul like suffering when accepted supernaturally. It is a most efficacious means of enduring our purgatory here on earth. Rejoice, all of you who cry and suffer and labor! You are on Calvary and hence closer to heaven and God. Impetrative power means that God cannot refuse a request from a soul that says, "I offer Thee my sufferings that Thou mayest give me Thy grace." Sanctifying power: no earthly beauty is comparable to that of a soul transfigured by sacrifice. That is how the Rosary teaches us to see pain. One savors it like a heavenly beverage, for in the bottom of this chalice we find Jesus and can say, with the Psalmist: *Calix meus inebrians quam praeclarus est*—"My chalice which inebriates me, how goodly is it!"[3]

Therefore, thanks to the Rosary, holiness is within everyone's reach. It suffices for us to model, in its Mysteries, all our actions on those of Our Lord. Should we endure physical suffering, let us join the unspeakable suffering of the Word Incarnate scourged at the pillar. If we must bear moral suffering, let us do so in the same spirit as He endured the Agony in the Garden and the Crowning with Thorns, which recall His moral suffering. As we practice an act of patience, let us keep in mind the ineffable patience of the Lamb of God carrying His cross to Calvary. Let it be a prayer that unites us to Him. If we have to study, let us reflect on the infinite knowledge of the Incarnate Wisdom revealing Himself to the doctors in the Temple in the fifth Joyful Mystery.

Children of Mary, Knights of her Honor Guard, the Kingdom of God is truly among you. You can become saints without resorting to multiple or extraordinary deeds. Your Rosary is the secret of perfection.

Meditate on the Joyful Mysteries, you men of sorrow and labor! You are working for eternal bliss. Unite yourselves with the Carpenter of Nazareth, saying, "O Jesus, Who were a worker like me, lighten my burden a little." You scholars who devote yourselves to study, why not stop for a moment and

---

raise your thoughts to heaven? To find repose, your bodily eyes, like those of your soul, need heaven. The eyes of the body are set on the visible skies; those of the soul need the sight of the heavenly Trinity that we invoke in the Rosary. Both soul and body will find repose in this simple prayer: "Our Father, who art in heaven, I offer thee my fatigue."

When the sweat of work or anguish floods your face, why not say to the good Master: "O Jesus, I mix my sweat with Thy bloody sweat in the Garden of Olives!" In this way, your day will be truly fruitful, and in the evening, you will be able to say, "Today, we have gathered treasures for heaven richer and more beautiful than our fields can yield." If suffering should visit you, and your face has more tears than smiles, then say, in the spirit of the Sorrowful Mysteries, "God of Gethsemane and Golgotha, I mix the blood of my soul to thy Blood, and my tears to thy precious tears as Thou redeemest the world."

Finally, we need the Rosary especially if our life is temporarily free from sorrow or suffering, as we can become blind and complacent. Voyagers of eternity, remember you are only wayfarers on this earth, which is not your final destination. The Glorious Mysteries will remind you of your supreme destiny. By recalling the triumph of Our Savior, the first Mystery will also remind us of the resurrection of the dead, that solemn and terrible day when the Angel of the Lord will cry out upon the ruins of the world: *Tempus non erit amplius!* "Time shall be no longer."[4]

In his solitude in the desert, St. Jerome imagined hearing the call of the last trumpet summoning the dead to Judgment. Meditating on the Glorious Mysteries will produce in us the same wholesome effect. As we watch the hustle and bustle of our big cities, let us reflect that all this worldly vanity, now so lively and vibrant, will one day lie in silence and death. Let us not stand on quicksand, as we are here one day and gone the next.

Let us hold fast to the Rosary as to an immovable anchor set in heaven and leading all the way to God. If we possess riches

---

[4]   Apoc. 10:6.

and pleasures, the Rosary will help us sanctify them, as it also sanctifies suffering and labor. Those who labor can recall the workshop at Nazareth; the afflicted can remember Golgotha, and those enchanted by the deceitful rays of worldly glory can remember the future glory of the triumphant resurrection and beatific vision.

Carved image of the Immaculate Heart of Mary in the Church
of San Miguel de los Navarros in Zaragoza, Spain.

Chapter Three

The Rosary and Perfect Holiness

Beyond the ordinary holiness necessary to enter the kingdom of the Holy Virgin, there is a nobler degree of sanctity that is still not the ultimate peak of the spiritual life but could be called the perfection of love in the perfection of sacrifice. It is holiness in the religious state.

Before ascending to heaven, Jesus Christ established two institutions in His Church, one destined to reproduce His role as a sanctifier and the other His personal holiness. The first is the priesthood, and the second is the religious state. Both must last until the end of time. Your sublime destiny, Oh, priests, is to perpetuate through the ages the mission of Christ as the sanctifier. Oh, men and women religious, it is your noble duty to reproduce the personal holiness of Christ.

When making their religious profession, consecrated souls pledge to aspire to perfection. In each one of them, God the Father must be able to recognize His Son, and looking at them, Mary must be able to say, they have the sweetness, charity, humility, and spirit of self-denial of Jesus. Now, to attain this stage of perfection, they must work incessantly at their sanctification, and even when making great efforts, they will not be able to say, "enough!" A voice in their souls will keep crying, "higher! higher!" Their model being Infinite Perfection itself, they must always increase their resemblance to Him.

Accordingly, religious life must be a continual advance toward perfection. Just what is that perfection? When we read the lives of great men and women religious, we see they paid the Church a tribute of heroism just as the martyrs paid the tribute of blood. Religious profession creates in the soul an ardent desire for perfection and a thirst for heroism, manifested more than once by sublime obedience.

Nevertheless, heroic charity is not the ordinary holiness demanded of the religious. It is higher than the charity expected of Christians in general, but it is a lower degree than heroic charity. What it does is remove all obstacles that might hinder the operations of divine love in the soul. It is a kind of perfect charity, or, as we said, the perfection of love in the perfection of sacrifice. Our Lord loved us to the point of sacrificing Himself for us. We reciprocate by dying to the world and sacrificing our worldly ambitions and possessions, dying to the flesh and senses through chastity, and sacrificing our will through obedience. When we immolate our hearts and souls and entirely give up to God our free will, a possession dear to even the lowliest children of men, then we have the perfection of love in the perfection of sacrifice.

A man or woman religious faithful to the three vows already has a perfect charity that borders heroism. However, to be faithful, merely avoiding mortal sin does not suffice. In a sense, a soul naturally remains in the state of perfection for as long as it avoids serious faults. Yet that inner voice keeps saying, "be perfect, go higher"—meaning, have a radical hatred of venial sin. Deliberately committing venial faults wounds our Blessed Lord "in the apple of His eye" and shows the person is not in the state of perfection of love in the perfection of sacrifice. Obviously, a serious desire for perfection must go hand in hand with the detestation of venial sin. Every step toward perfection is a victory against venial sin, and every time we deliberately commit a venial fault, we drop a degree from the radiant heights toward which a true religious soars.

Therefore, every soul earnestly desiring perfection must be resolved to avoid deliberate venial sin as much as possible. We say deliberate because the Church teaches that, save by a singular privilege such as the one granted to Our Lady, it is impossible to avoid venial sins throughout one's whole life. Furthermore, we do not make a vow to be perfect but only to work toward perfection. A person in the religious state who still has faults is not a hypocrite or liar except if he deliberately renounces his pursuit of perfection.

In short, religious holiness is to attain the perfection of love in the perfection of sacrifice, which supposes faithfully observing the three vows and having a profound hatred of every deliberate venial sin. To move toward these divine summits with a sure step, we must keep closely united to Jesus. Our Savior is the giant of eternity: If we keep holding His mighty hand, He will kindly take us by the hand and lead us on the royal way so we can exclaim with the Psalmist: *Exultavit ut gigas ad currendam viam:* "He hath rejoiced as a giant to run the way."[1]

The Rosary gives us the means to attain our goal. In the Rosary, Jesus is our model, our way, and our life. He is our model because He is the first and perfect religious of His Heavenly Father. He is our way as He gives us His almighty hand to sustain and support us, leading us to eternity. He is our life because these Mysteries pour marvelous graces into our souls to help us observe our vows. These are easy considerations, which we will be happy to explore.

In the Rosary, Our Lord is the religious *par excellence* of the Eternal Father. A man or woman religious is a person entirely bound to God. Indeed, the word religion derives from *religare*, which means to bind a second time. We are already bound to God by the indissoluble bond of creation and preservation, without which we could not exist for an instant.

Let us add to this physical bond a moral and voluntary bond. God is our first principle, and we adhere to Him by the bond of adoration. God is our sovereign master, and we bind ourselves to Him by submission and obedience. God is our ultimate end, and we unite ourselves to Him by the bond of love. Religion is the sweet chain that binds

---

[1] Ps. 18:6.

us a second time to our Redeemer and first principle. According to St. Thomas, all those who serve God may be called religious. Still, this name is usually reserved for those who consecrate their entire lives to the divine service and completely disengage themselves from worldly affairs.

The three vows, poverty, chastity, and obedience complete the task of attaching them to God. Poverty binds them to the source of all good; chastity, to a Virgin God, source of all beauty and purity; obedience, to God the King and source of all freedom. Thus, a man or woman religious is bound to God in every possible way.

In the fifteen decades of the Rosary, we admire the absolute submission of Jesus Christ to the will of His Father. In the first Mystery, the Incarnation, we see our adorable Savior assume our frail human nature and make Himself entirely dependent on God by becoming, so to speak, His vassal. Behold I come to do thy will, O God, He says: *Ecce venio ut faciam, Deus, voluntatem tuam.*[2] He said the same thing when about to return to His eternal abode: *Fiat voluntas tua* (Thy Will be done), the central thought of His entire earthly existence. When He left Mary and Joseph and stayed behind in Jerusalem, He did so to be about His Father's business. When He spent entire nights in ardent prayer, it was to fulfill the will of Him Who had sent Him.

He employed every instant of His life carrying out the mission entrusted to Him so that, when finishing His course, He could say, *Opus consummavi quod dedist mihi ut faciam:* "I have finished the work that Thou gavest Me to do."[3] He was the archetype of the perfect religious, entirely consecrated and bound to God.

How sweet it is to meditate on the Mysteries contemplating Jesus entirely dependent, poor, virgin, and obedient!

He practiced poverty to a heroic degree. He was born poor and remained so throughout his life, as He had nowhere to lay His head. On Calvary, the soldiers take His garments and divide them among themselves. To this day, He is even

2 Heb. 10:9.
3 John 17:4.

poorer by dwelling in the Eucharist, where He despoils Himself even of the appearance of humanity and dons the frail clothing of the sacramental species.

Concerning chastity, Jesus is a Virgin God, the Son of a Virgin Mother, and Spouse of a virgin Church. He willed His Body to be laid in a virgin, new sepulcher. He dwells in the Blessed Sacrament, the pure wheat of His chosen ones, the wine that produces virgins.

He had a passionate love for obedience, which made Him become incarnate, live and die, and then remain defenseless in the Eucharist, risking to be defiled by sacrilegious and apostate hands.

Hence, in all the Mysteries, Our Lord is the model for all religious, to whom He may say: "I have given you an example, that as I have done to you, so you do also."[4]

Our Lord is content with simply showing us the way. He is our way and our life. Meditating on the Mysteries of the Rosary powerfully communicates to us graces proper to our state in life. In the religious state, the three vows are a solemn challenge to the world's three major types of concupiscence. Our Savior overcame this triple power of the devil by His life, Passion, and Resurrection, which we recall in the fifteen Mysteries. While He Himself was never under the sway of this cursed concupiscence, He triumphed over sin for our sake by expiating the vices that originate in us from this triple root and meriting for us the graces of the opposite virtues.

Thus, meditating on the Rosary, we are watching the victory of Our Lord over the three types of concupiscence. This contact with the Word Incarnate will obtain actual graces for pious souls to overcome temptations and practice the opposite virtues. By uniting ourselves with poor Jesus in His different Mysteries, we receive grace to conquer the concupiscence of the eyes. Our contact with the Virgin Jesus will help us overcome the concupiscence of the flesh. Our humble obedience, modeled on His, will destroy the pride of life in us. In this way, observing our vows becomes easy,

---

4   John 13:15.

and we overcome temptations.

As we have seen, religious perfection does not consist in easily avoiding mortal sin but must include a lively hatred of the slightest venial fault—and the Rosary can obtain this grace for us. It will not only strengthen us in dangerous combats when our soul is at risk but also help us in our countless daily struggles against our unruly passions, lukewarmness, and earthly attractions. By placing us in contact with Our Lord, the impeccable archetype of all religious from His very birth, the Rosary enables us to receive a little of His admirable perfection and partake in the exquisite graces of His Sacred Heart.

These graces consist of forgetting ourselves and thinking only of our Well-Beloved and His interests, to fear above all offending Him in the slightest degree. The more we detach ourselves from ourselves and created things, the more we are attracted to lead a fervent life in the divine service.

Such are some of the choicest graces and marvelous effects bestowed on those who meditate wisely on the Rosary. Yet we must remain vigilant. If we fail to respond to His inspiration when He passes by, Jesus will be gone, and we will pursue alone our journey to eternity, a long and arduous path in which we can quickly become discouraged and fall back.

Therefore, let us always have recourse to Mary. In the Mysteries of the Rosary, we see how she practiced poverty, chastity, and obedience, so she knows from experience all the trials and troubles of a man or woman religious. She practiced virtues so perfectly as to exclude even a shadow of venial sin. If we unite ourselves to her in her celestial Psalter, the august Mediatrix of All Grace will obtain for us the grace to imitate her perfection, love of God, and hatred of sin. With Our Lady's help, we will strive to reach Jesus, and, for His Mother's sake, the good Master will deign to draw close to us again. Thus, in the company of Jesus and Mary, we will tread safely on our way to eternity.

If men and women religious only understood how to meditate on and practice the Rosary, how easy the way of perfection would become for them! Somehow, Jesus and Mary would lead them along the way with their graces so they would be able to say, like Brother Marie Raphael, O.P.: "In my Rosary, I have found the secret of holiness."

Mosaic of Mary Queen of the Holy Rosary on the facade of the Church of Saint Anthony in Vienna, Austria.

Chapter Four

The Rosary and Heroic Holiness

The degree of charity required of men and women religious is a sort of perfect holiness. However, the fecundity of the Church does not stop there. When nature has exhausted all its energies, and even grace seems to have reached its limits, it suddenly surpasses itself to such a degree that all things finite seem to disappear, leaving only the divine: it is heroism.

Heroism is a degree of virtue that stands halfway between the human and the divine—it is humanity transformed by divinity. As St. Thomas says, heroism renders men divine: *Secundum quam dicuntur aliqui divini viri.*[1] Heroism is the apex of sanctity. When giants of perfection pass through the world, we rise before them as manifestations of God.

From early martyrs to contemporary missionaries, the whole fabric of Church life is made of heroism. She has had twelve million martyrs! What a triumph of holiness! Whereas paganism and hell also reap their harvest of victims, the Church reaps a harvest of heroism. Every century has echoed the glorious cry of the early ages. A hero is one who subdues nature so completely as to sacrifice every other love for the sake of Jesus Christ. Every era has witnessed this prodigy. You see children imbibed with filial love and devotion wrenched from their parents' arms to follow a persecuted Christ and at times to die for Him. How bitter was that separation from home, giving up his father's caresses and seeing his mother's tears! But the

---

[1] *Summa Theologiae, Prima Secundae,* q. 58, art. I, ad I.

love of the Savior makes it sweeter and stronger, and turns His followers into heroes.

For its part, maternal affection quickly rises to sublimity by living on sacrifice and devotedness. History has seen mothers generously sacrificing their offspring for the love of Jesus. As a mother was about to be martyred, they took her child there to torture him. She placed her hand on his heart, telling him to be strong and hold fast to the Faith. "Because I love you more than myself, I offer you, my son, to suffer for Jesus. For the sake of your mother, come, my son, to die!" After her child, she walks joyfully toward death and thanks the Lord for kindly allowing her to make this double sacrifice.

Finally, you have conjugal love, in which two lives become one, the glory of which consists in chaste fruitfulness. In it, the spouses sacrifice their affections. Saint Alexis, Saint Elzear and Saint Delphine, Saint Henry and Saint Cunigunde, Saint Edward and Saint Edith sacrificed their hearts upon the virgin Heart of Jesus. In so doing, they reserved for their foreheads an immaculate crown, and the rose of Eden blossomed for them.

We have seen from the early Church down to our days, passionate souls enamored with Christ crucified, who gave Him everything and then their life and blood, saying: "O well-beloved, this is the language of our love: when love has given everything, it gives its blood, so here is mine!" All friends of the cross and heroic virgins repeated the triumphal hymn of St. Agnes, martyr: "I love Christ!"

Real heroism filled St. Paul's great soul as he wished to be anathema for his brethren. The same heroism inspired St. Vincent de Paul, the apostle of the poor, as he showed abandoned children in need to rich ladies of Paris, saying: "Their life and death are in your hands. If you have no mercy on them, you are condemning them to death!"

In the soul, heroism engenders a Christ-like love of one's enemies. It has led saints to kiss the bloody hand of their families' murderers. It led St. Louis-Marie Grignion de Montfort to cry, "O my God, take my life, but pardon my enemies."

Heroism still exists today, and it would be easy to cite names and significant episodes showing this burning love of God. It will last for as long as there is misery to relieve, love to give, and blood to shed.

While feeling unworthy of being named brethren of the saints, we must never forget that, in certain circumstances, every Christian may be called to heroism. By creating noble aspirations in our souls, baptism imposes grave obligations on us. Consequently, we may face in our lives struggles so tremendous that we will not overcome them merely with ordinary holiness: we will need energies from a higher level, and that is where heroism comes in. However, such extraordinary circumstances do not surprise the just. They are ready for great combats. Indeed, every soul in the state of grace possesses the blood of heroes, or rather, the seeds of heroism, which are the seven gifts of the Holy Spirit.

According to St. Thomas, these gifts do not differ from heroism. They are the seed of which heroism is the flower. The seed never blossoms forth into a flower in some souls, but the potential is always there. A harp is silent until a player touches it. All the seeds need is a sunray to open the bud. All a harp needs is someone to play it. This ray and this hand are the impulse of the Holy Spirit, which suddenly takes us over and leads us toward the sublime.

We must not ignore this beautiful doctrine out of misguided humility. However contemptible we may be, the "harp" of our souls, played by the Holy Spirit, can produce magnificent sounds. As we will explain, the Rosary will initiate us into this science.

Theologians teach that the Word Incarnate practiced every virtue to a perfect and heroic degree. Our Lord constantly lived off sublimity so that the story of His life became a history of heroism. Now, the history of Jesus is the Rosary. Heroism permeated and embalmed the entire series of Mysteries. It is there that the gifts of the Holy Spirit, hidden seeds in Our Lord's soul, budded forth into abundant flowers and the celestial harp struck those wondrous sounds that enchant humanity. Therefore, meditating on the Rosary suffices to contemplate virtue in its perfection and pinnacle, as all those predestined to heroism are to become like unto Christ Our Lord, Who reveals

Himself in its Mysteries.

This devotion truly is a school that forms saints.

A young knight named John Gaulbert set out one day accompanied by a large escort to avenge the murder of his brother. He caught the murderer in a vulnerable position, unable to escape. It was Good Friday, and the assassin extended his arms in the form of a cross imploring mercy for the sake of Jesus, crucified for us. In John's soul, that attitude aroused his latent germs of heroism. He not only forgave his enemy but also took him as a brother. As he entered a church shortly afterward, the crucifix inclined its head to thank him.

That is what the remembrance of a Mystery already did even before the institution of the Rosary. Indeed, the Mysteries are not only examples of heroism. They are particularly effective to make us practice their teachings. As we have often said, our union of soul with the Word disposes us to receive graces that can make us like Him. Our pious contact with the Savior's heroism will help us be heroic like Him. As it were, these choicest graces are like sunrays sufficient to make the seeds of heroism in our soul spring forth into flowers. They are like the touch that makes the harp, heretofore silent, give off a sublime sound. Then, divine breath breathes over our souls and leads us wherever it wants. At least for a few moments, our old faults and imperfections appear to vanish, fulfilling in us the words of Scripture: "Saul, too, has become a prophet." Thus, we can rise to the highest apex of sanctity simply by sticking to the Rosary.

Heroism is rather common in the annals of the Knights of Mary, and our readers may remember how it inspired the three Dominican Fathers, apostles of the Rosary, in their sublime apostolate during the sinking of La Bourgogne.[2]

That is not all. If heroism is a divine virtue, it must have a divine language, and God lends the heroes of sanctity a voice—the voice of miracles. The true Church has produced miracle workers in every age. Miracles were the thunder and lightning in the midst of which Our Lord promulgated the New Law. In the early centuries, they were more numerous because the

---

[2] Translator's Note: La Bourgogne was a liner of the Compagnie Générale Transatlantique, commissioned in 1886. It shipwrecked in 1898, killing more than 500 people.

voice of paganism still dominated that of truth. However, they are necessary for every epoch to manifest the holiness of the Church and convert souls. Unbelievers will always be around. We hear every day of unbelievers rising impudently against Christ and His Church in countries that have been Catholic for centuries. In His power and mercy, God silences these insolent revolutionaries by working miracles. To give only one example, in Lourdes, thunderous miracles force even the most incredulous to submit.

Miracles always happen in the Church, as Christ promised to grant them to every epoch and every people. "He that believeth in me, the works that I do, he also shall do; and greater than these shall he do."[3] These solemn words have been literally fulfilled. The Church has canonized and put saints on her altars in all eras. But she exacts from them the tribute of miracles, and the canonization process scrutinizes almost excessively the life of a would-be saint. Yet, saints keep paying the tribute of miracles after their death just as they paid the tribute of heroism during their lives. That is why, listening to her great voice, more powerful than rivers and seas, we exclaim, *Credo sanctam Ecclesiam*—"I believe in the sanctity of the Church!"

The Rosary teaches the practice of holiness and inspires a desire for heroism, but it has also been fruitful in miracles. As Pope Pius IX wrote, "Among all the devotions approved by the Church, none has been favored by so many miracles as the devotion of the Most Holy Rosary." Note that the Virgin of Miracles, Our Lady of Lourdes, is also the Virgin of the Rosary, who presents the Rosary to the people as a sign of hope.

The miracles worked by the Rosary have paramount social importance in that they constitute decisive victories for the Church, forever annihilating the power of evil. The Rosary's very first clash with Albigensian heretics resulted in their complete defeat. That is significant because, as a rule, great heresies are never overcome entirely by a single blow, but create problems for several generations after their authors are dead. However, the Albigensian heresy was destroyed immediately

---

[3]   John 14:12.

and entirely even though that powerful sect had the support of high-ranking clergy and laity. The institution of the Rosary completely confounded those heretics, and St. Dominic, while still alive, saw the enemy dying of its fatal wound without hope of recovery. Soon afterward, on the ruins of that heresy, France and the Church greeted the dawn of a bright future.

A few centuries later, the Rosary again clashed with Islam at the Gulf of Lepanto, bringing another victory for the Church. The Mother of God appeared in the skies, terrible as an army in battle array, encouraging the Christians and terrifying the infidels. Here too, victory was decisive: Mohammed's empire never recovered from this defeat and has since vegetated in powerlessness without recovering its former glory.

The Rosary has also clashed with the proud Protestant Reformation at the siege of La Rochelle, and the prestige of Protestantism in France has been ruined forever.

Such are great historical miracles worked by the Rosary. While we could cite many other miracles of healings, conversions that happen every day, our goal is to show that miracles and heroism are intimately joined in the Rosary as in the lives of the saints. The Rosary proves the holiness of the one true Church.

Although these miracles are due to the intercession of the Mother of God, they are worked in the Church and for the Church and illustrate the splendid aura that is the hallmark of her holiness and distinguishes her from all heretical sects. *Credo sanctam Ecclesiam*—"I believe in the sanctity of the Church!"

We now know how the Rosary, rightly understood, can initiate us into the various degrees of a perfect life. Let us ask Our Lady for the grace to understand these teachings. For, if we acquire this practical understanding of the Rosary, we will have conquered the science of the saints.